ENGLISH MIRACLE PLAYS

AND

MORALITIES

English Miracle Plays

AND

Moralities

BY

E. HAMILTON MOORE.

AMS PRESS
NEW YORK

Reprinted from the edition of 1907, London
First AMS EDITION published 1969
Manufactured in the United States of America

Library of Congress Catalog Card Number: 77-100517
SBN: 404-00598-5

AMS PRESS, INC.
New York, N.Y. 10003

FOREWORD.

The present volume is gratefully dedicated to those members of the Theatrical Profession who have attempted, during recent years, the revival of our early Drama. That this attempt has not achieved much more than a *succès d'estime* is not to be laid to the charge of those enthusiastic students and sincere artists who, at the cost of loss and disappointment, strove to re-awaken, to the light of modern day, the Sleeping Beauty of mediæval art.

Those who saw the presentation of *Everyman* by the Elizabethan Stage Society, of the *Chester Mysteries* by the English Drama Society, will not forget the reverent unclosing of that door, symbol-inscribed, and how long closed! through which came sounds and rumours of no fairylands forlorn, but the authentic voices of our own and Chaucer's fellow countrymen.

In an age like the present, it is well, now and then, to look back to the beginnings. The Theatre is a topic for all, a pastime for most, an experiment for some, a sincere enthusiasm for, alas, how few! The majority of those who deplore, the mass of those who defend its modern development, are equally ignorant of the processes by which it has been evolved, are almost unaware that such processes are implied.

What is a Morality? What are these Mystery Plays? Are they English or foreign? Who wrote them? Who

acted them, and how? What are they all about?—
These questions may be heard repeatedly even among
those who attend such performances as those already
mentioned.

To answer them as simply and intelligibly as may
be, and thus to help, in however small a degree, to
interest a larger public in the serious study of our
Theatre, has been the object pursued in the following
pages.

The book is intended mainly for those who have
neither time nor inclination for private research, and
is thus rather popular than scholastic, in view of which
fact, the majority of extracted passages have been
modernised in spelling and occasionally in phrase.

At the same time, for the benefit of those who wish
to further investigate the subject, a short list of the
best authorities on English Mysteries and Moralities,
will be found appended at the end of the volume.

                                        E. H. M.

I.

THE LITURGICAL DRAMA.

The Bible is the most dramatic book in the world, and its characters are the most splendidly pictorial and theatrical: Shipbuilding Noah, Joseph, the visionary statesman, priest-haunted Saul, beautiful, psalm-singing David the giant-killer, proud, painted Jezebel, Solomon wise and weak, dancing Salome, prophets and warriors, humble fisher-folk, virgins and Magdalens and nameless queens succeed and jostle one another in these pages as in life, and quickly as they pass us, we never forget them again. All life is there; its mysterious beginnings, its cruelty and greed, its ambition, national and personal, to which success is the smile of God, defeat, the desertion of Heaven; its joys and sorrows, its increasing perception of some deeper purpose out of ken of the present, something unknown, perhaps unknowable, in knowledge of which alone is happiness. How great, simple, and unconscious are the heroes of this narrative! How interested in life! To the Preacher even his ennui is worth experiment and record! How immense is their vitality that reaches us even to-day!

B

Wherever the Bible has been freely placed in the hands of the people it has become a folk-book, and its influence over the popular imagination would be difficult to estimate.   Every art has helped to foster this influence; music, poetry and painting have derived, and yet derive, great inspiration from their unwearied attempts to interpret and pourtray and illustrate even the most transcendent teachings as well as the actual records of the Scriptures; and there was a time when the dramatic, most living and most popular of arts, was recognised, not as a desecration, but as a legitimate and helpful exponent of religious truth. That time has passed : the religious theatre is no more.   How did it come to be?   What were its characteristics?   Why is it now among the things remembered or forgotten which are dead?   To these and related questions the following pages attempt some sort of answer.   There is only one form of answer possible : to tell the story of the Miracle Play.

The Miracle Play came into being at a time when the Bible was a closed book, and it sprang directly out of the service of the Mass. Very early plays exist, written on Scripture subjects : one by a Jewish author, Ezekiel, composed in Greek iambics shortly after the destruction of the Temple, and possibly intended to reanimate in his countrymen the ancient patriotism; another, the *Christus Patiens*, long but erroneously attributed to Saint

Gregory Nanzienzen, and like the first, on the model of the classics. These early dramas, however, in no way influenced the growth of the Miracle Play proper, and it is a mistake to regard them as origins. They are, at best, imitations of Greek Tragedy, and the Miracle Play everywhere, smacks of the soil.

It is quite possible that the Miracle Play would never have come into existence, if the services of the Church had been conducted in the vernacular; but they were, instead, conducted in an unknown tongue, symbolic language of things far from daily life, things beautiful, lofty, strange, yet dimly apprehended through the dramatic symbolism of the Mass. The altar is there, the victim, the broken body, the hush of death, the triumphant Alleluia. In itself the Mass is a drama, nothing easier than to illustrate it, to explain it to the popular imagination for which seeing and believing are the same. If the device seem childish, it is equally true that mysteries so transcendent can be grasped only by the childlike spirit, and the child learns best by pictures. The divinely ideal must submit to the interpretation of the material, the abstract of the concrete; symbol and sign spring up to shadow forth and finally to overshadow that which in its ultimate truth is inexpressible, capable of approximation, but not of entire appropriation by the mind of man. The announcements of Christianity, so daring and un-

familiar—how bring them into line with common
experience, daily life? Above all others, in a
world of change and death, that narration, of all
most challenging belief, of one who rose from the
grave! Death—consider what death meant to the
mediæval mind! Death the ineluctable necessity,
terrible and grotesque, partner in one grim trinity
with hell and judgment! He drives his levelling
chariot wheels over king, and pope, and kaiser;
in the cottage and the court, at fast and festival,
he shakes his castanets, the dread democratic
dancer. It passed belief—it passed, at least, experience, that any should escape him, and yet, something that was not only fear, hopefully answered
in the heart of man, the message that the conqueror
was conquered.

Thus it came about that Easter was the great
festival of the Church; instinct as well as faith
responded to the teaching of the day, and
Christian symbolism, grafted on Pagan tradition,
decked the empty grave with flowers once given to
Flora and to Freya. Out of the Easter Mass
sprang up the earliest liturgical drama, and it
sprang up spontaneously and instinctively all over
Europe.

In some of our ancient parish churches there
remain to-day stone structures, built into the main
edifice, and known to architects as *Sepulchres*.
One is to be seen on the north side of the altar in
Magdalen College Chapel at Oxford, now used for

the tomb of the founder, but serving originally a very different purpose. Parker, in his *Glossary of Architecture*, quotes from the annals of St. Mary Redcliffe Church for 1470, the bequest of a remarkably elaborate sepulchre made by one Canynge in July of that year to the vicar and " procurators " of the church. The sepulchre, in this case, was built of wood and richly gilt, with an image of God Almighty rising out of the same, a Heaven, belonging thereto, and made of timber and stained cloths, a Hell of timber and iron work, and Devils to the number of thirteen; four Knights well armed to keep the sepulchre, and four Angels with wings and wigs (*chevelers*), and the Holy Ghost descending from Heaven above. The whole suggests an elaborate tableau of the Resurrection, the only figures lacking being those of the Christ and the three Maries.

Long before Canynge and his bequest, the *Sepulchri Officium* had been established as part of the Easter service, its earlier and simpler forms dating probably as far back as the tenth century.

The ceremonial began on Good Friday, when the crucifix was taken down from the altar and laid in a sepulchre. An account of this, often quoted, is taken by Hone from an old book called *The Beehive of the Romish Church*, and is as follows:

Yea, and in some places they make the grave in a high place in the church, where men must go up many steps, which are decked with black cloth from above to beneath; and upon every step standeth a silver candlestick . . . and there do walk soldiers in harness as bright as St. George, which keep the grave till the priests come and take him up. Then cometh suddenly a flash of fire, wherewith they are all afraid and fall down, and then upstarts the man and they begin to sing Alleluia.

The *Beehive* is written in a critical spirit, and this account conveys none of the actual dignity of some of the earlier ceremonies. A thirteenth century MS., preserved in the Library of Orleans, contains ten of these liturgical dramas, written in Latin, and intended to be performed during the Church service. Among the rest is a *Mysterium Resurrectionis Domini Nostri Jhesu Christi*, dignified, simple and austere. It opens with a stage direction that (at a given point in the service) three clerks (*tres fratres*) dressed to represent the three Maries shall approach the Holy Sepulchre, singing, one to another in alternate versicles:

THE FIRST *of them saith.*

Alas! our Shepherd kind is dead,
Who blameless lived and sinless bled,
Oh heavy tidings!

THE SECOND.

Alas our Shepherd true is slain,
Whose holy life was free from stain,
Oh death, oh sorrow!

THE THIRD.

Alas for Judah's wicked seed !
What madness urged so dire a deed ?
Oh race accursed !
etc.

When also they come into the choir, they go
towards the tomb, as if seeking, and sing all together
this verse :

But who shall roll away the stone,
Too great for us to stir alone ?

To whom makes answer the ANGEL seated at the
entrance, at the head of the sepulchre, and clad in
white shining raiment, his brows girdled with a
crown, and bearing in the left hand a palm, and
in the right a branched candlestick, and saith in a
voice restrained and of exceeding gravity :

What seek ye in the sepulchre
O Christian folk ?

THE WOMEN.

Jesus of Nazareth, the crucified,
O heavenly one !

To whom answereth THE ANGEL.

What, Christians ! Seek the living with the dead ?
The Lord is risen, as to his own he said ;
Remember how he spake in Galilee
That he must die, but after ye should see,
Three days being past, his Easter victory.

Then the WOMEN, turning to the congregation,
sing :

To seek our Lord we came in tears,
An Angel sent from heaven appears,
And saith that he is risen.

All the episodes of the Gospel narratives follow,
the coming of John and Peter, the appearance of
the Gardener and the weeping Magdalen.   The
Angels utter their Alleluia :

Come, see the place where Jesus lay,
    Alleluia !
Nothing now your hearts dismay,
Change for joy your weeping cheer,
Christ, the living one, is here !
Hasten where his followers dwell,
Far and wide the tidings tell,
Jesus Christ is risen to-day,
    Alleluia !

Turning from the altar to the congregation, the
three Maries join the song in antiphonal response.
As their rejoicings ascend, he who had appeared as
the Gardener appears in the likeness of the Lord
(*in similitudinem Domini*), clothed in white and
glittering apparel, and turning to the women, bids
them :

Be not afraid; go, tell my brethren that they go
into Galilee, where they shall see me, as I declared
unto them.

THE CHOIR.

Alleluia ! The Lord is risen to-day !

THE RESPONSE.

The strong lion, the Son of God !

and THE CHOIR *saith*
Te Deum Laudamus.

At which point, probably, the service for the day was resumed.

Even a bare perusal of the original conveys to us something of the beauty and significance of the ceremony, played out in the gloom and glitter of a mediæval cathedral, the white-robed figures moving forward among the great pillars, under the glory of painted windows, through the mist of wafted incense, their voices chanting, antiphonal, in the beautiful Latin tongue.

Such Easter rituals—at first they were too primitive to be called plays—began to be general all over Europe from the tenth century onwards; later a dramatic presentation of the Descent into Hell came to be associated with the Good Friday and Easter spectacles, thus forming a complete three-day cycle.

The Descent into Hell, or the *Harrowing of Hell* as it was called in England, was one of the most popular of legends in mediæval times. It was a favourite theme of painter and poet, illustrated several times by Dürer, described by, among others, Langland, in *Piers Plowman*.

The original authority for the legend was the reference in the Epistle of St. Peter: *He went and preached unto the spirits in prison; which sometime were disobedient, etc.*, but this was greatly enlarged by the writer of the Apocryphal *Gospel of St. Nicodemus*, which narrates the whole episode in detail : How, as the Saints of Hell were rejoicing, there appeared in the darkness the colour of the sun, like gold, and a substantial purple light; and behold Satan, the Captain of Death, said unto the Prince of Hell, Prepare to receive Jesus of Nazareth; and the mighty Lord appeared, and visited those in darkness, trampling upon Death and overcoming the Prince of Hell, and taking Adam by the right hand, ascended from Hell, and all the Saints of God after him.

The subject was not only sympathetic to the mediæval mind, but in itself capable of dramatic treatment. The custom grew up to form a procession on Easter Eve, without the church. A certain door represented the gate of Hell, and was guarded inside, by a clerk—*in figura diaboli*. One representing Christ approached at the head of the procession, knocked, and demanded entrance. A parley followed in which the " Porter of Hell " was worsted, hell-gates were flung open, the victorious Lord entered, and rejoicing ascended. At a still later date, a new link was added to the chain, and the Walk to Emmaus formed the subject of an Easter Monday Mystery. In this way was formed the nucleus of a liturgic-dramatic cycle, which rapidly came to include every festival of the ecclesiastical year.

It is easy to imagine how readily the feast of Christmas lent itself to such symbolic ceremonial: a crib near the High Altar, a picture of the Virgin, two deacons, white-robed, representing the two midwives of Apocryphal legend, the shepherds advancing and kneeling, and the simple antiphonal responses:

What seek ye in the crib, Oh shepherds say?

The Saviour, Christ the Lord we seek,
The little child in swaddling bands.

To this day the crib is laid before the Virgin's shrine in southern lands, and Italian shepherds bring their offerings and pipe their songs before the new-born child. Of St. Francis of Assissi it is told that he let build such a shrine in the forest, and laid a living *Bambino* in the manger, watched over by ox and ass, and then summoned the country people to hear the Christmas Mass in that cathedral of green boughs.

The actual Nativity Play was, however, soon eclipsed by the Play of the three Kings, an episode capable of much more dramatic and decorative treatment. Simple as the Shepherds' Play in its

beginnings — the Kings met at the altar steps,
ascended them and greeted the Child—it rapidly
began to take on form and colour. From the
time when the character of Herod was introduced
the ritual became a drama, involving (supposed)
change of scene, and the play of conflicting
passions. We find a first sketch of the part of
Herod in a MS. of Nevers as early as 1060. Later
Herod became almost the most important of the
dramatis personæ. His rôle was that of a violent
egomaniac, subject to mad outbreaks of passion, in
one of which he commanded the slaughter of the
Innocents. The phrase to out-Herod Herod remains with us to-day, Hamlet's word for over-
acting. And indeed, the introduction of so in-
decorous a personage was not without danger, and
complaints early became common that the raging
of Herod risked the solemnity of ceremony. Perhaps for this reason a decree (of Bilsen) was passed
in the eleventh century ordering that such pieces
should be performed *after* the service, of which
they had hitherto been an integral part. Whether
the decree was locally obeyed is doubtful, but that
it should have been deemed necessary is in itself
significant.

Indeed the day was quickly coming when the
increasing vitality of the religious drama made it
impossible to retain as part of the service for the
day. Written at first by priests and monks in
Latin, of a character wholly symbolic and cere-

monial, the Miracle Play in so far as it dealt not
only with things supernal, but also with humble
shepherds, cruel soldiers and a proud king, touched
human life too closely to remain for ever cloistered.
And although the Easter and Christmas ceremonies continued long to be associated with the
service of the Church, other plays on similar
themes began to be written for performance outside the Church.

These plays were of two classes, afterwards confused, but at first kept quite distinct : *Mysteries*,
or Scripture Plays, and *Miracles*, plays dealing
with the legends of the Saints. As long as possible,
however, the Church retained her association with
both forms of drama, and the early Miracles and
Mysteries were still written in Latin and performed
in churches and in monastery schools.

The earliest Miracle, that is Saints' Plays, written
as distinct dramas and having no direct connection
with the services of the Church are supposed to have
been those of Hroswitha, a Benedictine nun of noble
family, of the Convent of Gandersheim in Saxony
during the reign of Otto the Great. Hroswitha
was a highly cultured, widely-read woman, her
sensitive mind cloistered and cramped to unnatural channels of thought, and her plays bear the
impress of her character. Ebert claims for her the
honour of being the earliest German poetess, but
this can hardly be conceded to one who wrote in
Latin. She left three volumes of her writings, two

containing poems on legendary and historic subjects, a third her six prose plays, written on a
Latin model, and exposing the glory of holy
chastity.   Whether these plays were ever acted
before the sisterhood within the cloister walls we
cannot say; certain it is that they could not, from
their   nature,   be   performed   without   them.
Hroswitha in avoiding Scylla fell upon Charybdis,
and her tortured spirit, shuddering from the fiery
contemplation of the impure, filled all the clearer
atmosphere with floating specks of darkness, and
with seared eyeballs blinked at images of evil, to
the natural man invisible.

Others, however, were writing less subtly and
more   sweetly,   among   whom   was   Hilarius,   an
Englishman and a student under Abelard.   France
claims our countryman, who was perhaps the first
to introduce into his Latin, tags and versicles in
the vernacular (c. 1125).   Hilarius has left three
plays—*St. Nicholas, The Raising of Lazarus,* and
Daniel and Darius.   His *St. Nicholas* is a good
illustration of the early Miracle Play.   It was performed on the feast of the Saint, when an actor was
dressed to represent the image of St. Nicholas, and
stood in a niche in the church.   To the shrine
came a wealthy heathen who, before taking a
journey, committed his treasure to the keeping of
the Saint.   But thieves entered, and on the
heathen's return the Saint stood guardian over a
rifled hold.   Furious, he took a whip and lashed

the image, which thereupon assumed life, descended, and accusing the robbers, bade them restore their plunder. As all are amazed at this marvel, lo, the inanimate image is once more silent stone, the Saint himself appears, and preaches Christ. The whole is typical of the mediæval mind, of that imagination which not only creates that which it desires, but equally eliminates what displeases it. To a modern, the moral might appear that a saint is set in one category with a woman, a horse and a walnut tree—but it was not so to Hilarius and his audience.

By the twelfth century we have *Le Drame d'Adam* written entirely in French, the first known vernacular Mystery, and from this date the secularisation of the religious drama kept pace with its popularity. The play of Adam is the first of which we know definitely that it was performed on a stage outside the Church, though the stage-direction that one of the actors shall make his exit by the church door at the back, proves the platform to have been placed against the church wall. The play dealt with the story of Adam, his fall and expulsion, and the sin of Cain, and was followed by a procession of the prophets foretelling the Messiah—a very favourite subject.

The name *Mystère* as differentiating the Scripture Play from the Miracle Play seems to have come into use in the fifteenth century, by which time secular drama had already its rude be-

ginnings in France. The term *Mystère* was later
dissociated from its original use, and was applied
not only to Miracle Plays, but to such dramas as
the *Mystère du siège d'Orleans*, and the *Mystère
de la destruction de Troie* which lie entirely outside the scope of our present study, and belong to
the story of the secular stage. In France the
drama developed early, and this may be in part due
to the fact that the Miracle Play preponderated
over the Mystery Play, and as Petit de Julleville remarks, the Miracle Play, with its more human
interests (for the saint is after all a man, and
must prove his claims by his life among his
fellows), appeals more intimately to the imagination
and to the inventive faculty, than the Mystery,
"condemned by its very sublimity to coldness, or to
a mingling of sacred and profane, unpleasing in
tone and finally scandalous."

This was indeed a prime factor in the decline of
the Mystery, at one time of a popularity incredible,
and infinitely greater than enjoyed by any other
form of drama before or since. All over Europe,
from Riga to Venice, among the Slavs and the
Dutch, Germans, Norwegians, Spaniards, the entertainment of kings, the piety of peasants, the ingenious resource of missionaries picturing for
primitive peoples the truths of the new faith,
everywhere, during centuries, the religious drama
exercised an influence which cannot be estimated.
There was an Easter cycle at Innsbruck, there were

Sepulchre Plays in Bohemia, with a patriotic prayer for the welfare of the people—*Da salutem Bohemis tuis*)—(Give salvation to thy Bohemians). In England no less than eleven towns had their Scripture cycles, played at Corpus Christi or at Whitsuntide. To-day we have one survival, the Passion Play of Oberammergau, while here and there some lingering ceremonial remembers bye-gone splendours—for splendid these representations came at last to be.

As the plays became more and more popular, the attitude of the Church gradually changed. The clergy were forbidden to take part as actors, and in some cases even as spectators, but on the whole the Church, if not always the Pope, remained sympathetic, and the performance was looked on as a work pleasing to God, and even efficacious in saving the city in which it took place from the ravages of the plague.

In 1264 a decree was passed definitely associating the performance of Mysteries with the feast of Corpus Christi, and it is from this time that we date the importance of our great English cycles, some of which yet remain to us in their entirety.

It is time indeed that we turn from the general study of the origins of the religious drama in Europe, to its early beginnings in England. Like many another noble and ancient lineage, our Drama also came over with the Normans.

c

NOTE.—In order to avoid confusion as to the terms *Mystery* and *Miracle,* a short explanation of their use may be here appended. In France, where the Bible Play and the Saint's Play flourished side by side, some distinctions of their functions might seem needed, but even in France the terminology was not exact. In England, where, oddly enough, the genuine Saint's Play had never the popularity of the Bible Play, the term *Miracle* appears to have been employed as a generic title for Church Plays of all descriptions. Contemporary references prove this. *Mystery,* on the other hand is a term of quite recent adoption applied to Bible Plays exclusively. In the present work this rule is followed, *Miracle* being used as a generic title, *Mystery* in definite reference to Bible Plays.

II.

CHURCH PLAYS IN ENGLAND.

In 1119 died, in the odour of sanctity, Richard, Abbot of St. Albans, and was succeeded by Geoffrey de Gorham, during some years a monk in that same cloister. The story told of Geoffrey's adoption of the cowl, as found in the *Lives of the Abbots of St. Albans* by Matthew Paris is as follows: At a certain time, probably during the last years of William Rufus, the Abbey School of St. Albans lacked a master. Abbot Richard opened negotiations with a layman, a Norman of illustrious family, cultured and virtuous. The post was accepted, and Geoffrey left France for England. In those days the journey was no trifle: unseasonable weather delayed the traveller, and he arrived, belated, to find the Abbey School in charge of another master. He settled at Dunstable, whence he could keep open negotiations with St. Albans, and partly to employ his leisure, partly, perhaps to prove his abilities, he set about the production of a little play on the life of St. Katherine. Probably it was meant as a school play for the Abbey School of which he had been promised the reversion, for we find him borrowing choir copes from the sacristy of St. Albans. Alas for the misfortunes of authors! On the night after the performance broke out by chance a fire, which

> Did consume both the house of Master Geoffrey, with his books, and the aforesaid copes. Not knowing, therefore, in what way to redeem to God and to St. Alban this great loss, he vowed himself to God's service, and assumed the habit of a Religious in that cloister. And for this reason, after that he was made Abbot of St. Albans, he did his diligence to let make for the Abbey, copes of price and beauty.

The Miracle Play of St. Katherine perished in the flames, and strangely enough, no actual Miracle Play, that is Saint's Play, has come down to us. That such were introduced, and for a short time popular, we have proof from contemporary documents. FitzStephen, a confidential servant in the household of Thomas à Becket, and one of those present at his murder, wrote afterwards a life of his patron and a description of London in his day, in which he refers to such plays as being common :

> London which hath for theatric spectacles and scenic dramas, plays of holier nature, representations of miracles done by holy confessors, and of that devout ardour by which the constancy of martyrs came to light.

Though the term *Miracle* is definitely associated by Matthew Paris and FitzStephen with Saints' Plays, its use was quickly extended to the Mysteries, or Bible Plays, which in England soon eclipsed the Miracles. While in French literature there are yet extant whole cycles of dramas, devoted entirely to the Virgin, in choice manuscripts, and gorgeously illuminated, the heroes of the Old and New Testaments appealed more strongly to the national taste in England; and so it came about that the Saints' Plays were early allowed to lapse, perhaps were never translated, and have survived only in passing, and rarely explicit reference.

We have seen already that the liturgical dramatic ceremonial connected with the celebration of Easter was common also in England. The exact date of its introduction is unknown, it was probably contemporaneous with the introduction of the more finished dramatic forms of Miracle and Mystery Play, for at the time of the Conquest all three forms existed side by side in France. Certainly there is no hint of any primitive drama, religious or secular, during the Anglo-Saxon period, and the genius of the Anglo-Saxon is too simple and austere to be compatible with any kind of mimicry.

The early Mystery Plays in this country were probably written by Anglo-Normans in Latin, Norman-French, and Anglo-Norman. When later the plays came to be translated into the vernacular, passages of Norman-French were sometimes left, embodied in the text. We have to remember that for some time after the Conquest the bulk of the population was bi-lingual. English was the language of serf and peasant, French of all cultured society. A middle-class jargon of Anglo-Norman touching both resulted, but it may be doubted whether abbot or baron would trouble or condescend to learn the language of the peasantry. There are parallel cases to-day, if less extreme.

The early authors of Miracles and Mysteries were Anglo-Normans, and we may assume them to have been clerics. Their authorities, the canonical and apocryphal Scriptures, were not accessible to laymen, and in an age of constant strife, the Church was the only assurance of leisure and learned hours. The literary faculty seems also to have been regarded as recommendation in the choice of tutor or private chaplain, and to have been accorded special privileges and emoluments. When the King came riding on horseback, and the Queen in a guarded litter, to spend a night and a day with some great lord, whose castle was shut in by waving boughs, or pre-eminent over wide, waste lands, it was well to have at hand some one who could improvise an entertainment, and with the aid of borrowed choir clothes pass an edifying hour. At Easter, too, and at Christmas, such plays were wanted for the private chapel, and certain items included in the *Household Accounts of the Earl of Northumberland (1512—1525) show how such performances were paid :

> If my Lord's chaplain be a maker of Interludes he is to have a servant for writing out the parts, else none. . . . My Lord useth and accustometh to give yearly to them of his chapel if they do play the Play of the Nativity upon Christmas Day, twenty shillings. . . . To pay for rewards to players for plays played at Christmas by *strangers* in my house, twenty pence every play.

The last item suggests a company of strolling players, but as we shall see later, the early Mysteries were not entrusted to such.

The first English Mystery Play extant, is a very crude piece of work, written in the East Midland dialect of the thirteenth century, and called *The Harrowing of Hell*. As a composition it cannot for a moment be compared with French plays of the same period, and it is difficult to believe that work so primitive is typical of all English plays produced up to that date.

The piece opens quite in the manner of the old romances, with their admonitory "*Listeth lordings !*"

> All hearken to me now !
> A strife I will tell you
> Of Jesus and of Satan,
> When Jesus was to Hell gone,

* In *Percy's Reliques.*

For to fetch forth his,
And bring them to his bliss.
The Devil had so much of might,
All must to Hell go—

Was none so holy prophet,
Since Adam and Eve the apple eat,
But at his life's end
To Hell pain must wend,
Nor might he thence come
Were not Jesus God's son.

.   .   .   .

Who, when He had shed His blood
For our need upon the Rood,
In His Godhead took the way
That to Hell-gate lay.
When He came there, thus said He
As I shall tell thee.

Here, probably, the speaker of the prologue withdrew, and Christ appeared before the yet barred gates of Hell.

Dominus.

Hard gates (*ways*) have I gone,
Sorrows suffered many a one,
Thirty-three winters less half a year
Have I dwelled in the land here,
Almost so much time is gone
Since I first became a man.

.   .   .   .

For Adam's sin full, ywis,
Have I sufferéd all this.
Adam, thou hast dearly bought
Thy sin, who didst obey me not,
I shall bring thee forth again,
With all mine own from Hell pain.

Here Satan challenges Christ—no stage direction
indicates whether the gate is at this point un-
barred. Satan has an ingenious argument against
the redemption of Adam. He is his property for
two good reasons, the first that he actually has
him in his hold, the second that in the beginning
he fairly bought him with an apple. Adam, he
says, was hungry, and for an apple I gave him,
swore me fealty for himself and his.

DOMINUS.

Satan, it was mine,
The apple thou gavest him.
The apple and the apple tree
Both created were thro' me.
How canst thou in any wise
Of other's goods make merchandise?

Foiled in casuistry, Satan becomes pathetic and
flattering. Surely, he says, thou art Lord of
all, and woe's him who denies thee. Be generous,
take power over Earth and Heaven—leave the
souls in Hell to me.

The inevitable end—so inevitable that the
dramatic interest can never have been thrilling—

is the overthrow of the Devil and the laying waste
of his dominions.   Prophets and patriarchs acclaim
the Christ, and the epilogue concludes, devoutly
praying :

> God for His Mother's love
> Let us never thither come !
> Lord for Thy much grace
> Grant us all in Heaven a place.

Innocuous as this appears to us the Mystery, or
as it was now indiscriminately called in England,
the Miracle Play, was already an object of Papal
suspicion and even censure.   Two decrees date
from the early 13th century forbidding the clergy
to make, see or take part in Miracles.   At the same
time, the reverent presentation of such mysteries
was encouraged as an act of devotion in laymen,
and in 1264 the performance of religious plays was
associated with the feast of Corpus Christi.   This
last decree was again confirmed in 1311 by the
Council of Vienne, and the plays were afterwards
frequently known as Corpus Christi Plays.

The decree prohibiting a reluctant clergy to
assist at such occasions was by no means observed
to the letter, especially in England.   In *Handlynge
Synne*, translated by Robert Mannyng, of Brunne,
from the French, in 1303, Miracles, tourneys, minstrel's tales, delight in horse and armour are
enumerated among those pomps and vanities of the
world renounced by the vows of the Church; but

the writer discriminates between Miracles played
out of doors for mere amusement, and those set
seemly forth in the Church for edification :

> It is forbade him in the decree,
> Miracles for to make or see,
> For Miracles if you begin,
> It is a gadding (*or a gathering*), a sight of sin.
> He may be in the Church for this reason,
> Play the Resurrection,
> To make men believe on God,
> How he rose with flesh and blood.
> And he may play withouten plyght (*blame*)
> How God was born in the holy night,
> To make men believe steadfastly
> That he was born of the Virgin Mary.
> But if it be done in ways or greens,
> A sight of sin it truly seems.

The French version runs—Another folly false
clerks have contrived—Miracles they call them :
their faces they with visor do disguise, which is
forbidden them in the decree—the worse their sin !

In *Piers Plowman's Crede* the Friar Minor cen-
sures the Carmelites on this score. They play the
Lulling of our Lady, that liketh the women, and
the Miracle of the Midwives. For ourselves, the
true Religious,

> We haunten no taverns nor hobble about,
> At markets and miracles meddle we never.

The clergy did, however, continue to take the

greatest interest in the arranging and producing
of the plays, and in their translation into English.
Without their supervision it is possible that dis-
orderly scenes must have early accompanied such
spectacles, which, on account of the great throng
gathered to see them, needed careful forethought
and planning.

There were also scapegrace clerks like Chaucer's
Absolon, who, to win the love of the carpenter's
fair wife, curled his locks and made him gay,

> And singeth, crowing like a nightingale,
> And sends her pasties, mead, and spicéd ale,
> And oft, to show his light agility,
> Playeth King Herod on a scaffold high.

At the time Chaucer wrote, such plays were
established as part of the national life, and his
Wife of Bath was one of an increasing congress of
pilgrims who crowded yearly to the towns where
the Corpus Christi shows were finest. It became
the custom, between the decrees of 1264 and 1311
to associate with the feast and procession of Corpus
Christi, the great festival of the Sacrament, not
only such plays as were directly connected with
the teachings of the day, but the whole cycle of
Scripture dramas, combined to form a sequence
from the Creation of the World to the Last Judgment. All these plays, the growth of many years,
the work of many men, coloured at last by as many
and as various influences as some weather-beaten,

lichen-covered rock, were brought into significant relation with the one central doctrine of the Church remembered upon this day.

A poem composed by Lydgate about 1420 gives us an insight into the inner significance of these plays. These fathers of the race, these patriarchs, prophets and kings, who seem to us of such individual interest, to the monkish mind are but types, precursors, and foreshadowings. Abraham, Sarah and the angelic visitant, in number three, are "figure only of the Trinity," and the bread which they break at their meal betokens the Sacrament of the altar. So with Melchisidec, Isaac, Moses and the rest. Receive these similitudes, he exhorts the audience, with due reverence, and be ever mindful of the Bread of Life, the celestial manna which is to sustain your passage from this Egypt, into the better world.

Fortunately, the secular mind was *not* mindful, and the lay figures took on life, pathos and humour, to the exceeding benefit of the national drama.

National it became, and in studying the English Mystery Play, we are studying, more than literature, the evolution of the modern world out of the old. We see the Drama, a living thing, leave its early home in the sweetness, the mystery, the shine and shadow of the Church and come into the streets, the ways and greens. We see it forgetting its early speech for the vernacular, the local dialect even; forgetting, too, its early authors, and grow-

ing, ever growing, as it goes from hand to hand—
growing in pathos, in imagination, in humour,
sometimes in coarseness, always in vigour and sap.
The priest stands in the background, looking on,
while the craftsman plays.   At last it passes away,
as a star fades in the dawn, or rather as the first
kindling sparks are extinguished in the greater fire
they stir.   But without such kindling there had
been no blaze.

Of the many cycles which were common all over
England during the thirteenth century, and which
began to be translated in the fourteenth and early
fifteenth centuries, four have come down to us,
more or less complete, those of Chester, Coventry,
Woodkirk and York.   Of other cycles we have
traces in single plays, while of the Cornish plays
known as Guaries, we possess also a perfect cycle.
A brief study of the great cycles, their history,
contents, and manner of presentation will suffice to
convey an impression of the performances all over
the country.   The Cornish plays need separate
mention later, for correctly speaking they come
only geographically within the limits of our title,
since the Cornishman is no Saxon but a Kelt.

III.

THE GREAT CYCLES.

The latter half of the fourteenth century saw
the translation of the Bible into the English
tongue, for those who were fortunate enough to
have learned to read; for the many to whom this
was an impossibility, the Bible was already a
familiar book, thanks to the nationalising of the
Theatre—the only Theatre—which was the religious one. The rapid growth of religious drama
all over the country was at this time phenomenal;
old Latin and French plays were put into the
vernacular, new plays were written in the English
tongue in all its variety of dialects. To us, looking
back on the period as a whole, there appears one
stream of tendency, watered by many springs, but
those who lived and wrought then, failed to per-
ceive the fact. Reform from the first separated
itself from the Theatre, and Wiclif himself was
an early instance of the narrowness of the Non-
conformist Conscience. The plays came under his
censure and those of his followers, and the playwrights retorted with a jibe at Lollards. He con-
sented, none the less, in pleading for a free translation of the Scriptures, to take a text from the

Devil, and thus we get one of our earliest references to the Mystery Plays of York.   Friars,
said Wiclif, have taught in England the Paternoster in the English tongue, as men see in the
play of York and in many other countries: since
the Paternoster, as clerks know, is a part of
Matthew's Gospel, why may not the other portions
be taught in English also?*

This *Play of the Paternoster* has gone the way
of another doctrinal drama, highly popular in
York, the *Play of the Credo*, long supported by a
large and enthusiastic guild or fellowship among
the citizens.   Both are but names and serve merely
to indicate the vitality of the interest aroused by
even the most abstract teachings of Christianity
when put into dramatic form.

But contemporary with Wiclif's reference there
existed in York the institution of a great cycle of
plays to be performed at the feast of Corpus Christi,
and of which forty-eight have come down to us in
a MS. of the early fifteenth century (the Ashburnham MS.).   To witness the performance of these
plays Richard II. visited York in 1397; for the
Corpus Christi play was to mediæval kings almost
what the race-meeting and bull-fight are to their
modern successors, and then as now, the presence
of the monarch drew additional crowds to the
festival.   At the time of Richard's visit, the plays

* *De Officio Pastorali, Cap. xv.*

had long since passed out of the four walls of the Church into the street, and were played in rotation, on movable stages called Pageants, which succeeded one another at various Stations in the town. The route to be taken by the pageants appears to have been a matter of much dispute, particularly about this time, when the first Station was at the Gates of the Priory of Holy Trinity, the monks of which house had then or later the property of what is now known as the Ashburnham MS. Various routes are mapped out from time to time in the city annals, for the greater convenience not only of the players, but of the crowd of strangers gathered to see the play, easily confused in the narrow, winding streets of the mediæval town. By 1417 the authorities seem to have despaired of a fixed route; probably as years went by, the character of districts altered and old landmarks were modified or removed, as in other towns; at any rate, in 1417, after a renewed attempt to direct proceedings, we find the suggestion that "those persons should be allowed to have the play before their houses who would pay the highest price for the privilege, but that no favour should be shown."

Twenty-nine years later it was found necessary to intervene again, owing to the boisterous character gradually acquired by the festival, and quite unsuiting to the original purpose of its institution, which was the honouring of the feast of Corpus Christi. Like many another custom, this was be-

D

coming " more honoured in the breach than in the observance," and it seemed advisable to separate the performance and the actual festival, to prevent any scandal from clinging to the latter.   In addition to the plays, there was, it seems, a procession supported by a Guild of Corpus Christi, and no doubt similar in character to that described in Lydgate's poem.   A Corpus Christi procession is, above all, a procession of the Sacraments, and such allegoric figures or tableaux as might be included in it, were meant to illustrate and typify the doctrine of the Eucharist.   That those who had just beheld with reverence, the passing of such a procession, should turn at once to scramble for places for the play, was in itself, unseemly, and the overcrowding of the streets by the production of the plays on their movable scaffolds or stages, while the procession was passing from church to church, was highly dangerous.   It was therefore resolved to separate the two, as follows :

Whereas for a long course of time the artificers and tradesmen of the City of York have, at their own expence, acted plays, and particularly a certain sumptuous play exhibited in several pageants, wherein the history of the Old and New Testaments, in divers places of the said city, in the feast of Corpus Christi, by a solemn procession, is represented . . . beginning first at the great gates of the *Priory of Holy Trinity* in York, and so going in procession to and into the *Cathedral Church* of the same, and afterwards to the *Hospital of St. Leonard* in York, leaving the aforesaid Sacrament in that place preceded by a vast number of lighted torches and a great multitude of priests in their proper habits, and followed by the Mayor and citizens with a prodigious crowd of the populace——

——A certain holy father, a Friar Minor, William Melton, observing that the play occasioned " revellings, drunkenness, shouts, songs and other insolences, little regarding the divine offices of the said day," whereby the indulgences granted by Pope Urban IV. (1264) for the good observance of Corpus Christi were in danger of forfeiture, advised, with the consent of the better part of the people, that the *play* should be performed on the *vigil* of the feast, and the *procession of the Sacraments* on the *day* of Corpus Christi, that all who came to see the play might have leisure to attend Mass and Vespers for their souls' health. This was done by decree of the Mayor and citizens on the 10th of June, 1426, Peter Buckley being Mayor of the city.]

The last performance of the cycle in York was in 1584, two years before the author of the *Arcadia* fell at Zutphen, four years before Shakespeare wrote *Love's Labour's Lost*. Elizabeth, but not Protestantism, viewed such plays with favour. In 1568, it had been already agreed by the City Council of York, that the book of the plays must be perused and amended before the performance, and there is little doubt that this was a concession to Archbishop Grindal of reforming tendencies. The manuscript actually bears traces of erasure and amendment to meet the approval of the new days and the new thought, while it is to this time that we have to ascribe the loss of the *Play of the Credo*. Submitted, by his request to Archbishop Grindal, the manuscript disappeared, and repeated requests for its return fell as vainly on episcopal as to-day they might on managerial ears.

From the nature of their verse and of their dialect, it seems improbable that the York Plays were translated from French or Latin. They are too intimately native and local for the supposition, and we can safely presume them to have been of English authorship from the beginning. The verse, infinitely more varied in metre than is usual in old French Mysteries, is closely related to the alliterative lines of early English poetry, and would in itself preclude the possibility of translation or adaptation. There are touches, too, of rude nature poetry here and there, quite unlike the nature poetry of the imported romances, wild, free, intimate, as the touches in our oldest lyrics. It is only in the York play that Herod, the braggart, praises his power and his person in terms of pure poetry: the clear clouds trailing one behind the other above his realm rejoice him, the thunder is his to throw, he can " rapely ride the rack of the red sky "; and speaking of his beauty, he does not say in the conventional phrase of the Towneley

Herod—"cleanly shapen, hide and hair, withouten lack"—but, with a soaring simile that paints a picture of wide, wheeling, sunlit wings, *I am fairer than glorious gulls, that are gayer than gold.*

Such touches, it must be confessed, are rare in the collection, but it should be remembered, that although written in one manuscript, in their present form, the plays are not likely to be the work either of one thought or of one period, and it is rare to find an ancient work of this kind, of the uniform character of the Chester Plays.

* * *

The York Plays form one group with those contained in, and often called after, the Towneley manuscript. This manuscript formed part of the library of Towneley Hall, Lancashire, and passed into the hands of the Towneley family with the tradition that it had once belonged to the Augustinians of the Abbey of Widkirk near Wakefield. The tradition stands alone, without witness, for or against. Widkirk, or, as we say, Woodkirk, lies four miles north of Wakefield, and formerly supported a cell of Augustinian or Black Canons. There is no reason why tradition should not be correct. The plays are in the north-country dialect, contain one or two local references to *Horbury* and the *Crooked Thorn*, which are in favour of the tradition, and have been in some instances strongly influenced either by the plays of York, or by some common original.   Like the York Cycle, they would seem, at least for the most part, to be of native growth, and like the York Cycle they are evidently of various authorship.   In the two collections five plays are practically identical: they are those dealing with the Israelites in Egypt, Christ among the Rabbis, the Harrowing of Hell, the Resurrection, and the Last Judgment.   In other plays there is wide divergence, and throughout the Towneley Cycle the Northern dialect is used in a less extreme form than in that of York.

This manuscript, of whose history we know so little, contains thirty of our most dramatic Mystery Plays.   For vitality, humour, and realism, no other cycle can approach it.   That no record of the performance of these living, sometimes daring, and highly popular dramas, should remain, is one of the mysteries of literature.   That the plays *were* acted is indicated by internal evidence, the apportioning of certain scenes to certain guilds, etc. Here the brief history of the cycle ends, and we must leave, for the present, consideration of its contents, to turn to the southern cycles of Coventry and Chester.

*

*   *

For as good hap would have it chance,
The Devil and I were of old acquaintance,
For oft in the play of Corpus Christi,
He hath played the Devil at Coventry.

Heywood's lines were written while the Coventry Plays were yet in their hey-day of popular fame, after enjoying many years of plebeian and royal patronage. Names of kings, queens and princes adorned the city annals of Coventry, recording through a long period the attracting power of her pageants. From the state visit of Elizabeth in 1574, surrounded with all imaginable pomp and circumstance, we can look back on the visits of Henry VII., in 1486 and 1492; of Henry V. and his nobles in 1416; of the little, ill-fated Edward, afterwards the fifth, as a three-year old child in 1474; of his murderer, then crowned Richard III., some nine years later; of Queen Margaret, who at the beginning of the troublous War of the Roses, came privately and with no pomp to Coventry, and would not be met, but was lodged at Richard Wood's, the grocer, and on the morrow saw *all the pageants played save Doomsday, which might not be played for lack of day.* This was in 1456. The preceding year had seen her with her husband, graced by loyal speeches, and by pageants of Hector and Alexander, Arthur and Charlemagne, which might seem prophetically meant to satirise or admonish the weak, incapable king, on the eve of civil war.

The history of the Coventry Plays is a curious one. There would seem at first sight to have been two cycles, one performed, as in other towns, by the Trade Guilds, the other by the Grey Friars of the city. Full records of the performance of Miracle Plays, of expenses incurred in costume and scenery, of special plays for special occasions, came down to modern times in the manuscript annals of Coventry. From these sources we derive our most detailed information as to the manner in which such plays were staged and represented, and the various manuscripts attracted the attention of antiquarian scholars at a comparatively early date. It is fortunate for students that they did so, and that they were in 1825 published by Thomas Sharp in his *Dissertation* on the Coventry Mysteries, for the originals themselves perished about half-a-century later in a disastrous fire in Birmingham. The accounts published by Sharp, refer to the plays " anciently performed at Coventry by the *trading companies* of that city," with no reference to the Grey Friars, and the two plays recovered and published in his volume were those assigned to the Shearmen and Taylors' Guild, and to the Weavers' Guild, portions, doubtless of a once complete cycle. At the same time we have another collection, consisting of forty-two plays, assigned at one time to the Grey Friars of Coventry, but now held to be of unknown origin. These plays are still referred to as the Coventry Mysteries, but with an understood query.

The manuscript in which these Mysteries are contained is a quarto volume of about 1468. In or about 1630 it became the property of Sir Robert

Cotton, and his librarian in cataloguing it, wrote on the flyleaf a note to the effect that the contents were the *Ludus Corporis Christi,* or *Ludus Coventriæ,* enacted formerly by the monks or friars mendicant. His authority for this note is unquoted and unknown, there seem to be no local allusions connecting these plays with Coventry, and modern philologists are doubtful as to the dialect. The truth may be that up to the time of the Reformation, the Grey Friars did not *perform,* which was " forbid in the decree," but largely *superintend* the plays produced by the trading companies, which were almost certainly of clerical authorship originally.

There is the more plausibility in this theory since the so-called Coventry Mysteries of the Cotton Manuscript can hardly be earlier than the fifteenth century, long before which period the clergy had ceased to appear upon the stage. The plays are thought to be of this date on account, partly, of the introduction into them of allegorical figures, such as Contemplacio, and the Virtues, which are rarer in early plays, though not in early poems.

These Coventry Mysteries, unlike those of York and Towneley, would appear to be translated from, or founded on Anglo-French originals. They are less popular in style, more scholarly in diction, more equal in merit, than the Northern plays, though they rarely rise to the same dramatic vigour. Their treatment of purely devotional

scenes is perhaps more dignified, and by their more
austere and religious character they compare
favourably with the other cycles in dealing with
such subjects as the Passion and Death of Christ.
Realism and rough humour in such connection can
only jar painfully.   On the other hand the real
human note is rarely sounded, and a singular lack
of combining power is shown in the treatment of
short episodes as complete plays.   In this respect
the authors of the *best* Towneley and Chester
dramas show a much better knowledge of the
capacities of their material, while the two sur-
viving Trade Guild Plays, printed by Sharp, con-
dense into their scope matter for more than half
a dozen of the *Ludus Coventriæ.*   Clerical authorship is proved not only in the undoubted literary
merits of these plays, but also in their constant
tendency towards edification.   An *Expositor* almost
invariably appears at the beginning, or during the
progress of the scene, masked sometimes as a
Doctor, sometimes as *Contemplacio,* sometimes as
one of the actors, and, directly addressing the
audience, exhorts, explains, and amplifies.   The
same tendency is characteristic of the Chester Cycle.

The Corpus Christi Plays, whether those of the
Cotton MS. or those of the Trade Guild Pageants,
or some others undiscovered, continued to flourish
until late in the sixteenth century.   In 1584 a new
play, now lost, was added to the list, the very
popular *Destruction of Jerusalem.*   But the end

was already in sight. Puritan divines were already teaching that pleasure is one with sin, and very soon the hoof of the joy-hating beast was set on innocent pastime. At a Council House held May 19th, 1591, it was unanimously agreed : "That the *Destruction of Jerusalem*, and either the *Conquest of the Danes*, or the *History of King Edward the Confessor*, at request of the Commons of this city, shall be played on pageants on Mid-summer day and St. Peter's day next in this city, and none other plays : and all the maypoles that now are standing in this city shall be taken down before Whitsun Day next, and none hereafter to be put up in this city."

With the maypole went the plays. The performance of these of 1591 is the last on record, and the city annals under 1628 refer to them as having been put down *many years since*—words whose sound seems haunted with faint, regretful echo.

*

* *

In the case of the Chester Cycle there is no doubt that the plays are translations or adaptations from French originals. Tradition says that the plays were instituted during the mayoralty of Sir John Arneway (1268—1276) and translated by Ralph Higden, author of the *Polychronicon*, who died in 1363 or 1373. Further, there is a note on one of the MSS. of this cycle to the effect that in order to obtain permission for the Englishing of the plays, Higden was forced to make three journeys to Rome.   This is picturesque and not improbable, and it is therefore somewhat disquieting to find other traditions associating the authorship of at least the English version, with one Randall Higden, and one Don Rondal, a monk, and yet earlier with one Sir Henry Frances, also a monk, who obtained from *Pope Clement* (which Pope Clement is not mentioned) one thousand days pardon for " every person resorting in peaceable manner with good devotion to hear and see the said plays from time to time."

The probability is that the plays were first composed, and later Englished, by monks of St. Werburg's Abbey in Chester, and that their performance received some definite impetus during the mayoralty of Sir John Arneway, at which time it must be remembered, the quite recent institution of Corpus Christi Day (1264) was giving fresh impulse to such performances all over Europe.

In Chester, however, while Corpus Christi Day was honoured by a solemn procession, the Mystery Plays were associated with Whitsuntide.   This is confirmed by the early Banes, Banns, or Proclamation which preceded the plays :

> Our worshipful Mayor of this Citie,
> With all his royal comunalitie,
> Solemn Pageants ordained hath he
>   At the feast of Whit Sunday tide.

How every craft in his decree
Bring forth their plays solemnlie,
I shall declare you briefëly,
    If ye will awhile abide.
        .   .   .   .

Also, master Mayor of this Citie,
With all his brethren accordingly,
A solemn procession ordained hath he,
    To be done to the best,
Upon the day of Corpus Christi;
The blessed Sacrament carried shall be,
And a play set forth by the clergy,
    In honour of the feast.

Many torches there may you see,
Merchants and crafts of this Citie,
By order passing in their degree,
    A goodly sight that day.
They come from Saint Mary's on the Hill,
The Church of Saint John's untill,
And there the Sacrament leave they will,
    The sooth as I you say.

This play set forth by the clergy in connection
with the Corpus Christi procession, was probably
either some liturgical drama in Latin, forming
part of the special service for the day and taking
place in one of the churches, or a series of *tableaux*
such as were frequently carried about in the procession, and representing prefigurative scenes from
the Old and New Testaments, typifying the doctrine of the mystical Bread of Life.   To such

tableaux it is probable that Lydgate refers in his poem quoted in Chapter II. It is not likely that the Chester clergy would break the decrees of the Church by taking part in plays, especially when there were thoroughly competent actors in the guilds.

The Chester Mysteries were performed on Monday, Tuesday and Wednesday of that week. The cycle is a comparatively small one, containing only twenty-five plays, some of which are peculiar to it. Like the *Ludus Coventriæ* it bears strong evidence of clerical influence, its general tendency being didactic rather than dramatic in intention. Here, too, we meet the Expositor again, and a strong appeal is made to the devout imagination. Plays on subjects not treated in other collections are such as appeared to their monkish authors peculiarly typical of the mission of Christ—they are *Melchisidec*, included in the play of Abraham, *Balaam and his Ass*, *Ezekiel and the Signs*, and *Antichrist*. It is also in the Chester Plays that we find the legend of *Octavien and the Sybil* in connection with the Nativity series.

The verse is throughout of very equal merit, and with the exception of some passages which Ten Brink considers the result of Chaucerian influence, is modelled on a French stanza usually employed in mystères and romances. It is much less alliterative than the verse of the Northern cycles, though alliteration is still employed. Collier in his *Annals of the Stage* has pointed out the strong parallels which exist between certain passages of the Chester Plays and early French Mysteries, and if further proof of the origin of the cycle were needed, it lies in the fact that there are, embedded in the text, and distorted by ignorant scribes out of all coherence, certain passages of what was once Anglo-Norman, or Norman-French. On the other hand certain passages recall the two Northern cycles. There is a resemblance to both the York and Woodkirk plays in the Chester version of *Christ among the Doctors.* Noah's wife, with whom we have later to form acquaintance, declares, in the York play, that she will not be saved alone, and let her cousins and gossips drown, a touch which is worked up into a really dramatic little episode in the Chester play. The beautiful passage in the Chester *Resurrection,* beginning,

> Earthly man that I have wrought,
> Awake out of thy sleep !
> Earthly man that I have bought,
> Of me thou hast no kepe (*care*).
> From Heaven man's soul I sought
> In a dungeon deep,
> My dear leman from thence I bought,
> For ruth of her I weep. . . .

occurs also in the Towneley play, and has possibly come to both from some other original. In this connection it may be mentioned here that the

Christ of the Coventry *Resurrection* exclaims in the moment of returning animation :

> Hard gates have I gone,
> And pains suffered many a one,
> Stumbled at stake and stone
>   Nigh three and thirty year. . . .

Lines so clearly borrowed from the old North-East Midland *Harrowing of Hell*, that they serve to illustrate the difficulty of ascribing to any single author, plays which grew slowly by oral and written tradition, absorbing into their structure so many composite influences.

Of the Chester Mysteries it only remains to add, that we are peculiarly rich in manuscripts, possessing five, between the years 1591 and 1607, proof of the extreme popularity of this cycle.

IV.

THE ACTORS AND THE STAGE.

We have seen that all over Europe the earliest theatre was the Church, the earliest actors were the clergy, that the representation was "grave, solemn and hieratic." How fared it then with the Drama when the tiring room was a green bush and Snout and Bottom enacted gratulatory pageants, and process-servers and bailiffs "Compassed a motion of the Prodigal Son?" Is Shakespeare's picture a true one, or does some spice of the professional's superiority over the amateur heighten his caricature? In short, what manner of actors had, in those days, their entrances and exits, on what stage, before the last oblivious curtain shrouded them and their art?

In France the Mystery and Miracle Plays became national property to a degree not attained in England, where the acting at least passed from the monopoly of one class to the monopoly of another. In France, especially in the provinces, priest and layman, noblesse and bourgeoisie, student and artisan, forgot all difference of rank (then so marked, that there was no danger of familiarity

E

breeding either contempt or spurious equality) to ensure the success of a common enthusiasm. If the clergy did not always actually appear upon the stage, they continued to encourage such performances as works of piety, pleasing to God, and efficacious in warding off plague. Dignitaries of the Church and wealthy lords contributed towards the expense of representations conducted on no small scale.

During the fifteenth century the association known as the *Confrères de la Passion* came into prominence in Paris, and obtained a practical monopoly of the religious drama in that city. As far as can be traced, this society had its beginning in the fourteenth century, and only ceāsed to exist after the first tragedies of Racine had been seen upon the stage. A full account of this Confrérie is given by Petit de Julleville in his *Littérature Francaise*: "They were the first," he says, "to possess a permanent theatre and periodical representations; a novelty which even from the beginning drew upon them certain vexations from the Provost of Paris." But Charles VI., with his famous Letters Patent of December 1402, ended these interferences, while conferring on them the monopoly of the representation of Mysteries in Paris. They played in the Hospital of the Trinity, which in 1539 they quitted for the Hotel de Flandres, finally settling, in 1548, in the Hotel de Bourgogne. At this moment was passed the

Arrêt of November 1548, by which the Court *a inhibé et défendu, inhibe et défend* to the members of the Confrérie to play *The Mystery of the Passion of our Saviour* or any other sacred mystery, under penalty, but permitting them to perform secular matters, *honnêtes et licites.* "We may say," adds Petit de Julleville, "that the *Arrêt* of November 1548, is the official date of the death of the religious theatre in France." It would appear that even prior to this date the original artisan and bourgeois class composing the brotherhood, had given place to professional actors, and from 1548 the history of the association becomes part of the history of secular drama.

Interesting as is the record of the Confrérie, typical to a certain extent of other such societies, the beginnings were quite different. Few guilds possessed a theatre or were under direct state protection. The favourite method of representation was on a fixed stage in the street. On such a stage, large enough to occupy the fronts of two churches, St. Saviour's and Holy Trinity, Henry VI. of England, entering Paris in 1431, was greeted by the pageant of the *Flight into Egypt.* When more than one play was to be performed, as in the case of a cycle, stages were erected at various intervals along the streets, and often scaffoldings for seats were placed opposite to them. These stages were of great extent, and as no curtain could fall to permit of change of scene, the stage itself was

broken up into various localities, each technically
designated a *Mansion*. Thus in the Passion Play
acted at Valenciennes in 1574, no less than eleven
places were represented side by side on the stage,
among which, Paradise with God in glory,
Nazareth, with a green field and a fence in front
of this quiet home, the Temple, Jerusalem, the
Palace, the Sea, Hell, with draconian jaws inviting
into the pit. Stage properties, machinery, costume
and music were on an equal scale, and the expense
lavished on such performances, at their best, must
have been enormous.

Nor were careful rehearsals forgotten. A proclamation exists for the rehearsing and performing
of a certain *Play of the Acts of the Apostles*,
quoted in full in Hone's *Ancient Mysteries*, and
again referred to in *Rymer's View of Tragedy*.
The date is 1540. Here we read how on a certain
day the banes of the play were cried by Heralds
at crossroads and public places, the announcement
being graced by a procession of trumpeters, buglers,
sergeants, archers, civic dignitaries in official dress,
and the managers of the Mystery—of whom the
names are given in detail; all which ceremony was
a preliminary not even as yet of the performance,
but merely of the rehearsal to be held on the Feast
of St. Stephen next following at the Hall of the
Passion, " the *accustomed place* for rehearsals and
repetitions of Mysteries played in the city of Paris,
which place, being hung with rich tapestry [and

furnished with] chairs and forms, is for the reception of all persons of honest and virtuous report."
Officers of justice were appointed to meet all
candidates at this Hall, carefully selecting those
most fitted to take part in the play.   The proclamation, in verse and prose, concludes with the
usual envoy

> Prince puissant, sans toy toute rencontre
> Est mal encontre, et nostre œuvre imparfaict . . . .

addressed to Francis I., in whose reign the brothers
Greban wrote their play, still extant in a black-
letter folio of 1541.

To further illustrate the extraordinary popularity
of such pieces, it may be mentioned that some time
later the *Acts of the Apostles* gave rise to a law-
suit, brought by the *Procureur Général du Roi* on
the one part, against *Francis Hamelin*, Notary of
the Chastelet de Paris, *Leonard Choblets*, Butcher,
John Louvet, Florist and Gardener, and *Francis
Pouldrain*, Tapestry-maker, on the other, and
accusing them of employing mean and unlettered
men to enact the Mystery, raising the price of
seats, and introducing so much of farce and
apocryphal history, that the plays were lasting
six or seven months, to the detriment of church-
going and general public morality.

*

*   *

The English took their pleasure, if not more sadly, more soberly and simply.   Perhaps some touch of lethargy suggested, in place of a series of fixed stages, which involved the tedious necessity of moving on for each new scene, the wheeled stage, drawn by men or, more rarely, by horses, which permitted the audience to remain stationary. Such stages seem to have been almost peculiar to England, though Creizenach mentions certain *Wagenspelen* (Waggon-plays) as being known in Holland.

While detailed pictures of French stages and performances have come down to us, we are obliged to reconstruct the English *pageant* from scattered items and suggestions.   Archdeacon Rogers, who died in 1595, wrote down an account of one of the late performances of the Chester Whitsun Plays, as witnessed by himself.   The pageant he describes as a high scaffold upon wheels, having two rooms, an upper and a lower.   In the lower the actors dressed, in the upper they played, and this was left open for all to see and hear, while the lower was draped with curtains or painted cloths.

Stands, he tells us, were erected at various points in the streets along the route to accommodate the audience.   The first pageant, beginning at the *Abbey Gates* " was wheeled from thence to *Pentice* at the *High Cross* before the Mayor, and before that was done, the second came, and the first went into *Watergate Street*, and from thence into

Bridge Street, so one after the other the pageants were played appointed for the first day, so likewise for the second and third day."

From a Proclamation made in 1415 in York we learn what precautions were necessary to ensure public safety and order in the crowded streets along which the pageant passed.

> No man save knights and squires of worship, that aye have swords borne before them, shall at that time bear any weapon, swords, or Carlisle-axes, and that they leave their harness at their dwellings. . . . Also that every player shall be ready for his pageant at a convenient hour, viz., at the mid-hour between the fourth and the fifth of the clock in the morning, and then all their pageants following ilk one after other without tarrying.

We cannot say whether Chester rose thus betimes.   Their shorter cycle had not to be compassed between one day's dawn and dusk, but lingered more leisurely over Monday, Tuesday and Wednesday of Whitsunweek.

As the lumbering vehicle passed down the street, its canopy of carved and gilded woodwork, cut into fantastic battlements and vanes, fluttering with bannerets, the waits went with it piping, some jester or tumbler might run to herald its progress, a cowled monk stood to watch with an archer from the greenwood—" lovely ladies here were lent," thronging their balconies, and the gay spring sun of an England that was merry, shone over all.

From items in the accounts of various Trade
Guilds, more especially those collected by Sharp,
and relating to Coventry, we glean our information as to costumes, stage properties, and other
details of the production.   From these too we
learn that waits and minstrels were employed to
enhance the performance and accompany the
songs.

Properties, few and simple, were for the most
part such as would now be supplied by the stage
carpenter.   For example :

Paid to Crowe for makyng of iij worldys . . . ij^s
Payd for settying the world of fyer . . . . v^d
Item : payd for kepying of fyer at hell mothe . . . iiij^d
Item : p^d for starche to make the storme in the
               Pagente . . . . vj^d

Among stage-properties we have also mention of a
barrel for the earthquake, a rope for Judas to hang
himself, a link for burning the world.

What manner of scenery could be crowded on to
the narrow stage it is difficult to imagine, but on
reading of such expences a^s thirteen pence " for
the matter of the Castle of Emaus," and frequent
references to the mending and stoking of Hell-
mouth, it is quite evident that the scene was not
merely enclosed with hangings.   The problem becomes more difficult in the case of such plays as
The Flood, or *Cain and Abel,* in the latter of which
Cain's entrance is made *plowing.*   In such cases

much must have been left to the imagination of the audience. In one instance only is there evidence that the actor felt himself to be "cabin'd, cribbed, confined," by the narrow compass of his stage, and this is the stage direction in the Coventry Shearmen's play—" Here Herod rages in the pageant, and in the street also."

The costumes were simple and traditional, but not at all historically correct. The Deity wore white, often white leather, and a gilt wig and beard. This costume served not only for the Creator but also for Christ, generally referred to in the items as God. Thus there are items for mending a cheveril (peruke) for God, and sewing of God's coat of leather and making bands for the said coat, twelve pence; also for painting and gilding God's coat and for a *Sudere* (Veronica handkerchief) for God. Saints wore gilded wigs and sometimes beards, nor were wings forgotten for the surpliced angels. Caiaphas and Annas went in bishop's rochets, our Lady had her crown. The tormentors or jailors of the Coventry plays had coats of black buckram with nails and dice upon them. The souls of the saved at Doomsday went in white, those of the damned in black and yellow, the colours of the Auto da fé. Herod had mask and helmet, and carried a *malle*, a club made of leather and stuffed with horsehair, and secured at the end of a stout stick. Most actors appear to have worn gloves, while an item of eightpence,

" paid to the painter for painting of their faces "
suggests an early use of grease paint.

But who among saints or sinners might vie in
impressiveness of aspect with the arch-enemy, the
Devil? Doubtless with the intention of increasing
the terror of his character, this personage was
decked like any medicine-man, and has come down
to us such a low-comedy figure, that we can understand his gradual transformation through the Vice
into the Harlequin.

The Chester Devil came on " in his feathers all
ragged and rent," while he of Gammer Gurton's
Hodge had " Horns to push, as long as your two
arms, with a long cow's tail, and crooked cloven
feet, and many a hooked nail."

Crying " *Harrow, harrow, out harrow!* " he
would leap upon the stage, a grisly mask on his
face, in his hand a staff or a *malle* wherewith to
belabour all who came in reach, sometimes a prong
or a fork for the driving of his victims into the
gaping jaws of Hell. His attendant demons were
only less fearfully presented, also disguised with
masks and bearing staffs, their coats made sometimes of leather, at others of coarse canvas, covered
with horsehair, hanging about them to give them
the aspect of hairy monsters. These frolicked
about their master at the Day of Doom, recounting
their services, the souls whom they had captured,
and their close fellowship with the Lollards, con-

sidered equal foes of Church and Stage. These
diabolic and impish characters, from being terror-
striking to the guilty soul, became rapidly burlesque, if in somewhat gruesome sort.   Perhaps
the most fantastic conception of the appearance of
the Devil is embodied in the stage-direction preceding the later morality, the *Castle of Perseverance*, the writer of which paid special heed to
the appropriate costumes of his characters :

> & he tht shal pley belyal, loke tht he have gune
> powd[er] brening in pypis in hys hands & in hys
> ers (*ears*) & in hys ars whane he gothe to batayl.

*

*   *

The actors of these plays were the members of
the various Trade and Craft Guilds. Their service
was perhaps less voluntary than is sometimes
imagined, as we find frequent decrees on the part
of the Mayor and Council commanding guilds that
have hitherto shirked a play of their own to join
with others, and petitions from other guilds,
craving, on account of their long service, for
exemption.   It would appear that the expences
were paid in the first place out of some general
fund of the guild enacting the piece, but when the
play came to be performed, the citizens contributed
freely to the show.   This was one of the grounds
of complaint of the Lollard preachers, and taking

for themselves the text that is associated with the keeper of the bag, they unconsciously endorsed its sentiments.   One such sermon preserved in a fourteenth century MS. at St. Martins-in-le-fields, complained with unconscious humour:

> This Miracle playing is very witness of men's avarice and covetise, that is *Maumetrie*, as saith the Apostle: for that they should spend upon the needs of their neighbours, they spend upon the plays; and to pay their rent and their debt they will grudge, and to spend twice so much upon their play they will nothing grudge. Also to gather men together to buy the dearer their victuals, and to stir men to gluttony, and to pride and boast, they play these Miracles; also to have whereof to spend on these Miracles, and to hold fellowship with gluttony and lechery in such days of Miracle playing they busy them before to more greedily beguile their neighbours in buying and selling; and so this playing of Miracles is very witness of hideous covetise.

The general expences of the play included not only the production, but the rehearsals, the writing out of the book, the maintaining of a pageant-house in which to keep the stage from year to year. We have items for the payment of actors for rehearsal and for playing, and the payment of the prompter or keeper of the book.   Thus among other items we find the following:

It' payd to God . . . . xxd*
It' payd to the demon . . . . xvjd
It' payd to the iij Maryes . . . . ijs
Item payd to ij wormes of conscience . . . . . xvjd
To Pilat hys wyfe . . . . ijs
To Fauston for cock crowing . . . . iijd

Also items of another nature which prove that
even in those days nothing could be done in England without much eating and drinking :

It' spent at the first rehearse at the brekefast of
    the companye . . . . vs viijd
It' spent at the ij rehearse . . . . iijs
It' payd for our soper at nyght . . . . iijs
It' payd to the dryvers in drynke . . . . . . viijd
Item : at Richard a Wood's dore for ale to the
    plaiers . . . . vd
Payd for a quart red wyn for Pilat . . . . ijd
Pd for alle when thei [the actors] dresse them . . . iiijd
Pd for o'r supper on the play day, for o'rselves,
    goodman Mawpas, the minstrull, the
    dresser of the Pagent, & the somnor &
    his wyfe . . . . iiijs

This was raising the tone of the profession indeed ! But not all men were allowed to sit round
that board. In England as in Paris great care was
taken in the selection of suitable actors, as may be

* This is surely for rehearsal only, as cf.—*Payd to
Robert Cro for pleaying God . . . iijs iiijd*

seen by the decree of the Council of York of the
year 1476, that

> Yearly in the time of Lent there shall be called
> afore the Mayor for the time being, four of the
> most cunning, discreet and able players within this
> City, to search, hear and examine all the players
> and plays, and pageants, throughout all the artificers
> belonging to the Corpus Christi play.   And all such
> as they shall find sufficient in person and cunning
> to the honour of the City and the worship of the
> said crafts for to admit, if able; and all other
> persons insufficient either in cunning, voice, or
> person, to discharge, remove and avoid.

It is perhaps needless to state that the stage was,
as yet, a masculine monopoly, a characteristic due
in doubt in part to its ecclesiastical derivation.
An exception in the case of the Chester Miracles
is pointed out by Dr. Joseph Bridge in his preface
to the three plays produced by the English Drama
Society :

> The worshipful wivës of this town,
> Find our Lady the Assumption,
> It to bring forth they be bowne (*bound*)
> And maintain with all their might.

Whether the good Ale-wives of Chester actually
appeared in the playing of their Pageant, we cannot say, but it is not quite impossible.

So the scene is set, the best of players are chosen, and the pageant begins its journey along the narrow ways. Let us mingle with the crowd and mark the play, learning what touched our forefathers to tears and laughter, and to what lays the minstrels piped ghostly, forgotten music.

V.

COMEDY AND TRAGEDY.

The plays, it must be repeated, were the people's Bible, and in a two-fold sense. The Bible of Wiclif, circulating, under censure of the Church among his own adherents, could hardly reach the lower strata of society for whom reading was an unknown science, and the parish priest a known and formidable authority. On the stage the Book was opened as nowhere and no time else. And the Book was the people's Bible in as far as its rendering was entrusted to their hands, inasmuch as their own sufferings, their own joys, grew vocal between the lines of ancient story. It was not always possible. Clerical influence and tradition had set apart the Miracle Play as a means of grace, a spectacle for edification. Too often these living men and women of old Palestine and Syria become abstractions, types, no longer children of men but mere changelings of priestcraft, colourless and faint. Especially is this the case in those cycles in which the purpose is most definitely instruction, but even in these there are varying degrees of merit. It may be thought that the

F

introduction of such symbolic characters as Melchisidec, or of such prophetic characters as Balaam, and Daniel, presented not as character-studies, but as foretelling the Messiah, is fatal to dramatic art. It is so, but thanks, probably, to the trend of popular taste, such personages are rare.   Shipbuilder Noah and his scolding spouse, plowman Cain, the troubled father Abraham, good Joseph, the carpenter, wed with too young a wife, the Shepherds, simple men and puzzled by angelic Latinity—such are the favourite characters, most dramatically portrayed and most intimately realised.   The instinct which selected them was probably unconscious.   Of democratic thought the plays are innocent, only in one or two of the Towneley Cycle, the protest of class against class, the ancient, modern cry of the burden bearer pierces our ears and dies down; but this is rare, so rare, that in reading it we instinctively recognise the fact that the play had for author a *man*, a personage, who wrote out of his heart, with a clean pen on new parchment, and did not merely correct and revise the work of forgotten clerks.   One of John Ball's way of thinking, but more resigned to fate must have written thus :

But we simple shepherds, who walk on the moor,
In faith we are near hands out at the door;
No wonder as now stands, if we be poor.
While the tilth of our seed lands lies bare as the
    floor,

As ye ken !
And we are so lamed
So driven and shamed
O'ertaxéd and tamed
By these gentlery-men !

Thus they reve us our rest—Our Lady them harry !
These men are lords fast, and for them the ploughs
tarry !
Folk say, All for the best ! but we find it contrary
Thus are husbands opprest in point to miscarry
Their lives !
Thus hold they us under,
Thus bring us in blunder,
Great is the wonder
If one of us thrives.

Since the limits of the present work forbid any
close comparative study of the contents of the four
cycles, it is perhaps best to consider such episodes
as serve to illustrate the realism, humour, pathos
and poetry to be found in these dramas, choosing
by preference those plays which are to be found in
all the cycles, the most popular, presumably, with
the audiences of the day.

For realism in its most developed form we turn
to the Towneley Plays. While the *Cain and Abel*
of the Coventry Cycle is a dim and lifeless symbolism of the death of Christ, while the Chester
play is unrelieved tragedy centring so closely
about the guilt of Cain, that Abel hardly appeals
to us at all, the Towneley play is simply and frankly

a play of murder.   Here and here only the dying
Abel cries to heaven for vengeance, while the
tragedy is increased by a grotesque attempt at
comic contrast.   Note too how we are prepared for
some outburst of passion on the part of Cain from
his first entrance.   He is plowing, and as he plows,
cursing his horses.   Calling to his boy he accuses
him of having underfed the animals and appro-
priated their corn.   The boy, introduced as the
buffoon, laughs in his face and vaunts his fault
with pride, whereon :

CAIN.   I am thy master ; wilt thou fight?
GARCIO.   Yea, with the same measure and weight
That I borrow will I quit.

At this moment Abel enters with an ill-timed

God as He both may and can,
Bless thee brother, and thy man.
CAIN.   As welcome hadst thou stayed without !
Thou shouldst have bide till thou wert called !
Come near, and either drive or hald.

Abel's business is, however, not plowing, and
he breaks it to his brother :

Our father us taught, our father us kenned
That our tithe should be brenned.
Come forth, brother, let us gang
To worship God, we bide full lang.

Give we Him part of our fee,
Corn or cattle, whether it be,
And first cleanse us from the fiend
Ere that we make sacrifice,
Then His bliss withouten end
God will grant for our service.
    CAIN.   What gives thee God to praise Him so?
He gives me naught but sorrow and woe.
Yea, wherefore should I tithe, dear brother?
Hear my truth, it is none other,
Each year am I worse than other.
My winnings are but mean,
No wonder if I be lean.
And He has ever been my foe,
For had He my friend been,
Other gates had we seen :
When all men's corn was fair in field
Then was mine not worth a neeld.
When I should sow and wanted seed,
And of corn had full great need,
Then He gave me none of His,
Neither give I Him of this!

Appearing to yield, he kneels beside his brother, whose brief and simple thanksgiving is barely uttered when Cain's harsh voice breaks in upon his worship :

Rise! let me now since thou hast done.
Lord of Heaven, hear my boon!
And God forbid there be to Thee
Love or gratitude from me.
For as I go on two shanks,
It is full sore, and with no thanks,

The tithe that here I give to Thee,
Of corn or aught doth nourish me.
But now begin will I then,
Since my sheaf I needs must bren:
One sheaf, one, and this makes two,
But neither of these can I forego.

The grudging pile of mildewed and rotten
sheaves being collected he sets a light to it:

Woe, out, harrow! help to blow!
It will not burn for me I trow!
Oh, what Devil of Hell is it?
Almost had my lungs been split!
Had I blowën one blast more
I had been choked right thore (*there*).

ABEL.   Cain, this is not worth a stroke,
Thy tithe should burn without this smoke.

CAIN.   Go to the Devil and let me be!
It burns all the worse for thee!
I would that it were in thy throat,
Fire and sheaf and every sprout.

DEUS.   Cain, why dost thou so rebel
Against thy brother Abel?
Thou shouldst neither chide nor flyte,
For meed is his whose tithe is right,
And surely if thy tithe be false
Only ill to thee befalls.

CAIN.   Who was that that piped so small?
Get we hence for perils all!
God is out of His wit!

Then turning on his brother:

Abide! we have a crow to pull!
Hark, speak thou with me ere thou go!
What! Weenest thou to escape me so?
Nay, nay, I owe thee foul despite,
And now is time I thee requite.

ABEL. Brother, why hast thou so great ire?

CAIN. Come, thief, how burned with so bright fire
Thy tithe, while mine, the while, but smoked,
As if it would us both have choked?

ABEL. God's will I trow it were
That mine brenned so clear.
Why thine smoked am I to say?

CAIN. Yea, but thou shalt sorely pay.
With this jawbone, ere I slake,
I from thee thy life will take!
Lie down there and take thy rest!
Thus shall shrews be chastised best.

ABEL. Vengeance! Vengeance! Lord, I cry,
Who am slain and not guilty.

DEUS. Cain, where is thy brother Abel?

CAIN. Why askest thou me? I trow at Hell,
At Hell I trow he be:
Who so were there, he might see—
Or somewhere fallen on sleeping.
When was he ever in my keeping?

DEUS. Cain, Cain, thou wast wud!
The voice of thy brother's blood,
That thou hast murdered in false wise,
From earth to heaven for vengeance cries,
And for thou hast brought thy brother down
I give thee here my malison!

CAIN.   Yea ! deal about thee, for I will none,
Or take it thee, when I am gone !
Now I have done so mickle sin
That I may not thy mercy win,
And thus thou puttest me from grace,
I shall hide me from thy face.
And where so any man may find me
Let him slay me hardily—
Where so any man me meet,
On the hill or in the street.
And certainly when I am dead,
Bury me at Guid Bower at Quarrelhead !
No matter ! I know where I shall go,
I shall have a place below,
It is no boot for mercy crave,
For if I ask, I shall none have.

Reprobate and hardened to the end he whistles
to his boy, and tells him, with a blow, what he
has done.   Master, says he, we shall have the
bailiffs on us !   And as Cain announces to him and
to the audience the terms upon which he now lives,
the boy mimics him behind his back :

CAIN.   I command you in the King's name.
GARCIO.   *And in my master's false Cain!*
CAIN.   No man with us find fault or blame.
GARCIO.   *My master has cold roast at hame!*
CAIN.   The King writes you until . . .
GARCIO.   *I had never yet my fill!*

Come down ! exclaims the impenitent, and to
the Devil with you.   I never knew your match
except that brother Abel of mine !

As he resumes his plowing, the grotesque little episode closes, and it is difficult now to say in what manner it was intended to impress the audience.

Concerning the play of *Noah* there can be no such question. Whence sprang the tradition that Noah's wife was a scold, a vixen, a shrew without a tamer?

> Hast thou not heard, quoth Nicholas also,
> The sorrow of Noah and his fellowship,
> That he had ere he got his wife to ship?
> He had well liever, I dare well undertake,
> At that same time, than all his weathers black,
> That she had had a ship herself alone.

In the Coventry Cycle only is Mrs. Noah the dully, dutiful echo, who knows that her man knows best. In the York play, the Chester, and the Towneley, her individuality and vivacity of temperament are depicted *crescendo*.

In the first of these, the goodman shows an amount of tact which hints a large experience. Not a word does he say till the Ark is built and the flood already rising. Incredulous at first, she breaks, on conviction, into not unnatural reproaches: You might have let me know! Early and late you were off to the forest and never said a word, while I might sit at home. . . . Hold me excused Dame! It was God's will, says he. So you think we are quits! she retorts, nay, thou

gets a clout, by my troth! Pray be still, cries
Noah, ducking, I've been building it a hundred
years. Come, say the sons, father's making a far
flitting, you must in :

> Be merry, mother, mend your cheer,
> This world be's drowned withouten dread !

With difficulty she is induced to enter, crying
loyally that it is unfair that she should float while
her cousins and cronies perish in the flood. Her
family fail entirely to sympathise with her, and
thank Heaven for their own dry skins.

This last really lovable touch in the woman's
nature forms the kernel of a dramatic little episode
in the Chester version. Noah's first suggestion,
put, a little unwisely, in the form of a command,
that his wife should into the Ark, has been met
with a refusal, and the poor man wrings his
hands :

> Lord, but women are crabbéd aye,
> And never meek, that dare I say !
> This is well seen by me to-day,
> In witness of you each one.
> Now, good wife, come, change thy cheer,
> For they all ween thou'rt master here,
> And so thou art, by St. John !

> WIFE. Yea, sir, yea! Set up your sail,
> And row you forth with evil bale,
> For withouten any fail,

I will not out of this town,
But I have my gossips, every one;
They shall not drown, by St. John,
An' I may save their life.
They lovéd me full well, by Christ!
And, but thou let them in thy chest,
Row forth, Noah, where thou list,
And get thee a new wife.
    NOAH.   Shem! son, thy mother is angry! lo,
Such another I do not know.

Leave her to me, replies Shem, and approaches, politically, with no better result than a somewhat milder answer:

Son, go again to him, and say
I will not come therein to-day!
    NOAH.   Come in wife, a twenty devils' way,
Or else stay there without.
    HAM.   Shall we *all* fetch her in?

Meantime the flood is rising, and as its waves begin to lap on the doomed shore, the Good Gossips break into song:

The flood comes in full fleeting fast,
On every side it spread full fare,
For fear of drowning I am aghast,
Good Gossip, let us draw near!
And let us drink ere we depart,
For oftentimes we have done so,
For at a draught, thou drink'st a quart,
And so will I do, ere I go!

Here's a pottle of Malmsey, good and strong,
It will rejoice both heart and tongue,
Tho' Noah think us never so long,
Here will we drink alike!

The Towneley play, is as usual, more detailed.
As Noah is soliloquising on the wickedness of the
world, God warns him of coming disaster. I thank
Thee, says Noah, for troubling about such a simple
knave as I am. I pray only my wife be not angry
when I tell her. . . . God speed thee, dear wife,
how fare ye? . . . As I may: the worse for seeing
thee! Where hast thou been all this time, while
we swink and sweat at home and have not food to
eat? . . . Wife there is ill news to-day. . . . There
is always ill news with thee! God fulfil it on
thine own head! He knows the life thou leadest
me. A curse on all ill husbands. But I can requite mine enemy, for I know how to smite and
smile. . . . Hold thy tongue, or I'll make thee!
. . . Come on then! . . . Ay, have at thee! . . .
Take that! . . . Ah! wilt thou? That was mine!
. . . And there are three knocks for two.

Presently she begins to cry, and he draws off, half
scolding, half admiring. There is, after all, no
one like her, mutters Noah, she can bite and whine,
strike and skrike. They part on better terms, she
to spin and to pray for him, he to build the Ark,
hard work for his old bones. He has not yet dared
to mention it to her. When at last she learns the

truth, she is for a moment startled, but the critical
and sceptical spirit being strong, she begins to jeer
and to doubt. This is more of Noah's madness, and
as for the Ark,—In faith, says she, I cannot find,
which is before and which behind! At least she
will spin out her yarn. Noah is alarmed:

> Behold to the Heaven! The cataracts all
> That are open full even, both great and small,
> And the planets seven have left their stall!
> The thunder and levin gar down to fall
>   Full stout,
> Both halls and bowers,
> Castles and towers:
> Full sharp are these showers
>   That rain about.

As, after considerable delay, his wife consents to
enter, the opportunity to lash at her from behind
with a whip, proves too much for Noah's prudence.
He yields to this temptation, with natural results:
Spare me not, I pray thee! Thy great words cannot flay me! Cry me mercy! . . . Not I! . . .
Then will I break thy head! . . . Lord! were I at
ease and happy of heart, a poor widow-woman with
her mess of porrige! How gladly would I pay the
mass-penny for thy soul! aye, and so would many
another wife I wot of! Such lives husbands lead
us! . . . Ye men that have wives, while they are
young, if ye love your lives, chastise their tongue!
A second battle follows, and a second reconcilia-

tion. As their sons rush to separate them, with
exclamations of horror, Dear bairns, says weary
Noah, pathetically, we shall do your bidding and
be wrath no more; now will I take the helm . . .
and therewithal Noah and his whole family enter
into the Ark and fall to praying, in great terror of
the storm.

Pathos follows hard on mirth in the play of
Abraham and Isaac.   Here again the Coventry
version loses a little by comparison with the
others; in fact in all the plays except the Towneley
one, Isaac is too resigned to his bitter fate, too
much a symbolic figure to excite our deepest
emotion.   In the Chester play this resignation is
not without touching sweetness.   It is Abraham
who hesitates and trembles, the boy who entreats
him, for pity, to make an end.   Use as few strokes
as may be, says Isaac, when you smite off my
head!—grim recollection of the headsman's axe.
Bound on the altar he bids his father farewell, and
sends a greeting to his younger brothers :

And pray my mother of her blessing,
I come no more under her wing,
Farewell for ever and aye !

What ill have I done you? cries the Isaac of the
Towneley play, defiant, entreating for life.   Have
mercy and think on your child !   When I am dead

and closed in clay, what son will you have then?
No—only let me speak first! Only put up your
sword! It dazzles me! I do not know how I
have sinned! Think of my mother, spare me for
love of her! The water shoots in both my eyes,
says Abraham. If he had been once unkind it
would have been easier. Surely it is a sin to kill
him thus and be for ever haunted by his rueful
words! What shall I say to his mother? She
will ask at once, Where is he? If I say he has
run away, she will not believe me, and I shall be
her death too! How still he is lying there, not
daring to stir till I come! Oh could I cease from
weeping till the deed were done!

When the Angel appears to warn him—I thank
God, says he, but to speak with thee I have no
leisure till I have spoken with my dear son. He
runs and kisses him. . . . Is all well, and may I
live? I was almost mad with fear!

*

* *

Poetic sentiment clings like an exquisite fragrance to all the legends of the Mother of Christ:

When I thus had wed hir thare,
We and my maydens home can fare,
     That Kyngys daughters were.
All wroght thay sylk to find them on,
Marie wroght purple, the oder none
     Bot othere colers sere.

Do not these lines from the Towneley Plays summon up such old-world pictures as William Morris loved to weave in tapestry and in verse? The whole legend of the Virgin, as treated in these mediæval plays, how charming it is, how remote from all necessity for criticism, how full of suggested light and perfume, rosy wings of angels, tall white lilies, swinging censers!

Naturally, we turn for the fullest exposition of this legend to that cycle of plays which is in character rather devout than popular, always a little mystical and symbolical, the *Ludus Coventriæ*. At this point we have no longer four, but five variants before us, those of Chester, York, Towneley, and in addition to the *Ludus Coventriæ*, (the *so-called* Coventry Cycle) those two pageants, *really* of Coventry, to which we have already referred. These deal exclusively with the birth and youth of Christ, and must be mentioned in connection with the others.

So much importance was attached by those responsible for the *Ludus Coventriæ*, to this portion of sacred history, that it was preceded by a special exhortation uttered by *Contemplacio*, setting forth its contents and praying:

Christ conserve this congregation,
From perils past, present, and future;
And the persons here playing, that their pronunciation
    tion
Of their sentence to be said might be sad and sure,

And that no interruption make the matter obscure;
But may it profit and please each person present,
From the 'ginning to the ending so to endure,
That Christ and every creature with the conceit be
  content.

The Feast of the Tribes is come, and the good
Joachim would fain present himself before the
altar with his brethren. But Anna his wife,
albeit her name means Grace, has borne him no
child, a sign of divine displeasure, for which he
may be repulsed at the altar steps. None the less,
after taking a touching leave of the weeping Anna,
he sets forth with his offering to the Temple. As
he enters, the priests before the altar are singing
the *Benedicta sit beata Trinitas*, and swinging
their censers. Trembling he draws near, only to
be repulsed and dismissed out of the place. As he
stands apart the words of the service come to him :

Adjutorium nostrum in nomine Domini,
Qui fecit coelum et terram

and he sees his brethren depart, rejoicing and
signed with the Cross. He thinks sadly of his
wife. It will break her heart if she hears of his
reproach, he cannot see her suffering. He feels
exiled from her fellowship and turns aside, seeking
the company of shepherds, in whom is " little
pride." They welcome him gladly : their life is
free from care, their flocks are pastured wide, the

G

ewes and the lambs together, increasing and
multiplying, blessed of Heaven : And you master?
How fare you? You look heavily! And our good
dame—does she sit at home at her sewing?

To hear thee speak of her doth slay my heart!
God knows how we do fare, both she and I.

Seeing that their talk has touched some trouble
they desist, only promising to pray for him " in
what simple way as we know." Joachim falls on
his knees, and while he is praying we see Anna,
left at home, waiting and praying for him. To
him comes an Angel, singing, *Exultet coelum
laudibus*, and promises that his wife shall bear a
child, Mary, who shall be dedicated to God and
become the Mother of Christ. Have ye had good
tidings, master? Then we be glad! says the
shepherd, seeing his face, and Joachim answers
him, Praise God for me, for I am not worthy.

Meantime the Angel messenger has greeted
Anna also, and she hastens to meet her husband
at the Golden Gate :

Now blessed be our Lord, and all His works for ay!
All heaven and earth must bless you sure for this.
So glad am I as never words can say,
There is no tongue can tell what joy within me is.
I to bear a child that shall bear all men's bliss,
And my husband have again—who might have joys
    more !
No creature on the earth is more mercy shown, lives,
I shall hie me to the Gate that I may be there before.

The next scene opens when the little Mary, now three years old, is presented in the Temple, but all life and dramatic interest are crushed out of sight by the symbolism and mysticism with which the action is invested, and we pass on to that favourite topic, the *Bethrothal of Mary and Joseph,* a theme which even the Coventry playwright could not divest of its touches of pure comedy.

The maiden Mary being of legal marriageable age expresses her intention to live all her days in pure virginity, to the great perplexity of the Bishop in whose Temple she has been dedicated. Unwilling to violate either the law of the land or the girl's conscience, the Bishop and his clerks seek direction from on high, singing, *Veni Creator Spiritus.* The answer is an Angelic admonition to summon all the kinsmen of the House of David, bidding them bear white wands in their hands. Whose wand breaks into blossom, let him wed her. The proclamation, cried throughout the land, comes to the ears of the old man, the carpenter Joseph, himself of the royal line. The proclamation amazes him, but he at least is not concerned. It were "a strange thing for an old man to take a young wife," and for one whose failing steps require a staff to present himself at all in such an assembly of suitors. Only superior force can frustrate his intention to hide, and he is compelled to join the rest. Dragged ruthlessly forward into

public view, the poor man's age takes on Methusalen
proportions :

> I am so agéd and so old,
> That both my legs begin to fold,
> I am nigh almost lame.

Required to lay his wand before the altar he
answers that he cannot. It is "mislaid." There
is always, on these occasions, an officious friend,
and so it is with the hapless and protesting
Benedict-Joseph, whose wand is found, and found
in radiant bloom. He breaks into lamentation :

> What! should *I* wed? God forbid!
> I am an old man, so God me speed,
> And with a wife to live in dread,
> It were neither sport nor game.

> An old man may never thrive
> With a young wife, so God me save,
> Nay, nay, sir, let be.
> Should I now in age begin to dote,
> If I her chide, she will clout my coat,
> Blere mine eye, and pick out a mote,
> As oftentimes we see!

Married he is none the less, when his troubles at
once begin. The tender bride, the serene beauty
of whose person no laughter mars, must have
handmaids to attend on her, and a fitting home to
dwell in. Come, says Joseph, now in part re-

signed, I have hired for us a pretty little house for you and your damsels to dwell in. For myself, I must now into a far country, and work to maintain for all. I shall return again in nine months, see that you live discreetly.

The *Salutation* follows, and next *Joseph's Return*, the substance of which latter play may be imagined. The women in some of the cycles tell him that his wife has been visited by an Angel in his absence: An Angel, cries the justly outraged man! Doubtless *she* thinks him so, but tell *me* of no Angels!

Reconciled at last, he is ready to fall at her feet and crave her pardon, before setting out with her to visit cousin Elizabeth and her good husband.

This *Visitation* is a delightful piece of writing and breathes an atmosphere kindly, homely and essentially bourgeois throughout. It resembles the picture of some Flemish painter—the motherly Elizabeth, important and affectionate, the younger Mary, devout and tender bride, the mutual womanly confidences on expected events, the meeting of the old men, at once elated by their prospects of paternity and aware of their own quite secondary importance.

Well, darling, how are you? says Elizabeth, and Mary answers, I have been wanting to see you for a long time, I know you too are hoping for a child . . . . Ah, how do ye, how do ye, father

Zackary? cries Joseph, we are both ageing fast!
Well, why are you shaking your head? Have you
the palsy, sir, or can't you speak? No offence
taken, I trust!

This episode is followed in the Coventry series
by a curious and disagreeable scene to which, in
other cycles, there is no reference at all, the *Trial
of Mary and Joseph*. The subject, the arraign-
ment of Mary before the Bishop's Court for
incontinence is taken from apocryphal Scripture
and the whole incident is treated with a
license of language alien to the general tenor of
this collection, and extremely repulsive and painful. The dramatic interest of the piece lies in the
introduction of non-scriptural characters Backbiter and Raise-Slander, while the Prologue to the
piece has a distinctly satirical interest, and is
worth quoting from :

Avoid, sirs, and let my lord the bishop come,
And sit in the court, the laws for to do,
And I shall go in this place them for to summon :
Those that be in my book, the court ye must come to.
I warn you here all about,
That I summon you, all the rout,
Look ye fail for no doubt,
    At the court to 'pear !
Both John Jurdon and Geoffrey Gyle,
Malkyn Mylkedoke, and fair Mabyle,
Stevyn Sturdy, and Jak-at-the-Stile,
    And Sawdyr Sadelere.

Cok Crane and Davy Drydust,
Luce Lyar and Letyce Littletrust,
Miles the Millar, and Colle Cakecrust,
 Both Bet the Baker and Robin Red!
And look ye ring well in your purse,
For else your cause may speed the worse!
And tho' ye sling God's curse,
 Even at my head, come fast away,
Both Bouting the Brewster, and Sybil Slinge,
Meg Merryweather, and Sabin Spring,
Tiffany Twinkeler, fail for nothing—
 The court shall be this day.

Before discussing the various Christmas or
Nativity Plays, it may be better to bring to a close
the story of Joseph and his domestic troubles. In
most instances he sinks into the usual insignificance
after the birth of the Child, but in the pageants of
the Coventry Trade Guilds his less acquiescent
character is drawn with a rare fund of quiet
humour. He is still resentful, still a little jealous.
The time comes when the Child is to be presented
at the Temple, and according to the dramatist who
has combined several incidents into one sequence,
this event takes place almost at the same time as
the finding of the Child among the Doctors. Before
leaving home, Mary approaches Joseph, and with
little coaxing endearments, requests him to procure
her two doves:

There shall be no doves sought for me, says
Joseph. I pray thee, dame, leave these jests and
talk sense. Am I fit for birdnesting?

Aye, dame, aye!   God help us all,
Methinks your memory is but small,
On me so rudely ever to call!
You nothing mind mine age.
But the weakest aye goes to the wall;
So go thyself, dame, for me thou shall,
Or else get thee a new page.

How say ye, all this company,
That be wedded as well as I?
I ween that ye suffer much woe!
For he that hath wedded a young thing,
Must fulfil all her bidding,
Or else may he his hands wring,
Or water his eyes when he would sing,
And that you all do know.

Despatched to the forest he wanders to and fro,
grumbling and whimpering and falling into the
hedges, till a pitying Angel catches him the doves,
and sends him dancing home.

Now Mary will be satisfied:

I am full glad I have them found!

No mention of his wife's old friend, the Angel.

Am I not a good husband?
That am I, so may I thrive!

God reward you, answers the merciless woman,
we can start now for the Temple. . . . What, at
once?   And not blow awhile, and I working all
day?

Lo my friends, here may ye know
The manner of my wife is so,
That with her I needs must go,
    Whether I will or nill.
Now is not this a cumbrous life?
Lo, what it is to have a wife,
Yet rather than to live in strife,
    I must e'en do her will.

Take up your child, Mary, and truss up your gear. It is I who have to carry it, I know, and now let us walk together.

In his heart he adores the Child, and praises it to all strangers, so pretty, so obedient, so forward: *It is early sharp that will be thorn.* None the less, when the Child is found to be missing he is not eager to return, and invents a score of reasons for proceeding quietly home. Fie, what tales! says Mary. Arrived at the Temple, the good Carpenter declines to enter. He could never talk to the gentry, and there they are in a row, all clad in their fine furs—Go in dame, you have the better tongue for such as these.

The treatment of this Temple scene serves to illustrate the way in which the plays grew up from common sources and influenced one another. It occurs almost word for word in the York and Towneley Cycles, and it is not now possible to trace the direction of the influence. With this play we lose sight of the home life of Mary and Joseph. At the foot of the Cross, at the gate of the grave, the maiden Mary is become the Mater Dolorosa, and in such plays as deal with the *Death of Mary*, the *Assumption*, the *Appearing of our Lady to St. Thomas*, all humanity, gracious or sorrowful, is gone, and we stand in the presence of a cold abstraction, for which laughter and tears are stilled, and from which, however devout an inspiration may proceed, it can be in no sense of the dramatic order.

But we have yet to stand beside the manger cradle of Bethlehem, and with the Shepherds under starry skies.

VI.

THE GOSPEL STORY.

(1)

As I rode out this other night,
Of three jolly Shepherds I saw a sight,
And all about their fold a star shone bright,
They sang, Terli, terlow!
So merrily the Shepherds their pipes can blow!

Down from heaven, from heaven so high,
Of Angels there came a great company,
With mirth and joy and great solemnity,
They sang, Terli, terlow!
So merrily the Shepherds their pipes can blow!

(2)

The other night so cold,
Hereby upon a wold,
As Shepherds watched their fold
In the night so far:
To them appeared a star,
And aye it drew them n'ar (*nearer*),
Which star they did behold,
Brighter a thousandfold

Than the sun so clear
In his mid-day sphere,
And they these tidings told.
      What, secretly?
      Nay! hardily!
They nothing did conceal,
For there they sang as loud
As ever shepherds could,
Praising the King of Israel!
   Yet I do marvel
In what pile or castle,
These herdsmen did him see!
      Neither in halls nor yet in bowers
Born he would not be;
Neither in castles nor in towers
That seemly were to see.
But at His Father's will,
The Prophets to fulfil,
Betwixt an ox and as
Jesu this King born was.
Heaven he bring us till!
      But when these Shepherds had seen him there,
Into what place did they repair?
      Forth they went, and glad they were,
Going they did sing;
With mirth and solace made good cheer,
For joy of that new tiding.
And after, as I heard them tell,
He rewarded them full well,
He grant' them Heaven therein to dwell—
In are they gone with joy and mirth,
Their song it is Nowell!

          *

   *   *

In the plays relating to the Shepherds and the
Star, that tone of gentle, tender familiarity, which
can at once be playful and devout, that intimate
intercourse between the human and the divine
which so sweetly presumes the relations of child
and father, or at times of servitor and lord as to
appear the absolutely natural attitude, and the
most reverent, reaches its climax.   These plays,
and those relating to the Magi, remind us of some
old pictures.   The divine Child clings to his
mother, a little shy, the charm of human childhood
brighter than the halo round his brow.   Good
Joseph smiles benignly and indulgently, the
Shepherds who have come to worship a God, look
up to remember their little ones at home, or the
child long since grown to manhood and departed.
The Kings in rich raiment and cloth of gold, do
not draw so near in spirit as these, humbler and
simpler; though we remember the Flemish masters,
and particularly that rare *Adoration* of Malines, so
human, so touching, the huge Negro, succumbing
to the divine influence, kneeling, timid, and awe-
struck, his attention, which in the Antwerp picture
is rivetted almost too gallantly on the mother,
arrested by the child.

So in these plays is the same mingling of what
we differentiate as human and divine.   The
Shepherds are not Eastern sages, their lives are no
better and no worse than those of their neighbours.
They are very plain English peasants and the best

tenders of sheep "from comely Conway unto Clyde." Their meal consists of Lancashire jannocks (*i.e.*, oatmeal bread), Halton ale, butter, cheese and black puddings. When the Star appears to those of the Chester play they are engaged in a quarrel with their lad, who accuses them of stinting his wages, while they retort that he is insolent and idle. The appearance of the Angel is by no means received "on the knee," but with alarmed bewilderment and a momentary suspicion that here is some new kind of sheep-stealer or spy. When, in one of the plays, a Shepherd wiser than his fellows begins to expound the prophets as to the coming of the Messiah, they quickly silence his "clergy" and plainly think he is bragging of his learning. Arrived at Bethlehem, their offerings are touchingly simple, and their remarks almost too naïve.

> Sim ! Sim ! Sickerlye,
> Here I see Mary,
> And Jesus Christ fast by
> Lappéd all in hay !

They are much struck by Joseph's appearance and great age :

> Whatever this old man here is,
> Take heed how his head is hoar !
> His beard is like a bush of briers,
> With a pound of hair round his mouth, or more.

Says another : Whoever he be, he is a heartless fellow and only heeds his heels. He is greatly in need of a nap ! . . . Nay, says a third, he is right heedful to his wife, the worthy wight, only his beard hides his face.

They make their offerings—a little bell for the baby, a flagon and a porrige spoon, a cap, " a pair of my wife's old hose, for other joys, my son have I none to give thee." The boys who have followed the Shepherds also bring their gifts :

> Oh, noble Child of thee,
> Alas, what have I for thee,
> Save only my pipe ?
> Else truly nothing,
> But were I the rocks in
> I could make this to pipe
> That all the woods round ring
> And quiver as it were.

> Now, Child, tho' thou be come from God,
> And God thyself in thy manhood,
> Yet I know that in thy childhood,
> Thou wilt for sweet meats look :
> To pull down apples, pears and plums,
> Old Joseph need not hurt his thumbs,
> Because thou hast not plenty of crumbs,
> I give thee my nuthook.

The most important and interesting of all these plays, is the death of Pilate in the *Resurrection.*

found in the Towneley collection.   Going far beyond the scope of the usual Mystery, this is in truth
our earliest comedy, and much better work than
such later pieces as *Gammer Gurton* and other contemporary specimens of Comedy.   So great is its
importance as to necessitate more than passing
reference.

The piece opens with the lament of the poor
Shepherd already quoted, and the philosophic re-
flection :

> It does me good as I walk by mine own,
> Of this world to talk in manner of moan.

To him enters a second Shepherd, complaining
of bitter weather and keen frost.   But worse than
weather is wedlock, he begins, and plunges straightway into the ocean of his troubles, marvelling that
those who are free are so little mindful of the
example of those who are bound :

> But now late in our lives, a marvel to me,
> That I think my heart rives, such wonders to see,
> (Save what destiny drives, it needs must be)
> Some men would have two wives, and some would
>   have three
>   In store !
> Some are woe that has any,
> But so far ken I—
> Woe is him that has many,
>   For the more is his sore !

On this monologue comes a third Shepherd, Daw, whose complaint of the great floods might help to fix a date for this piece. In addition to the floods he has another grievance, one that gives a vivid touch to the wide, wild, winter night—namely the strange sights that scare poor shepherds when other men's eyes are closed in easy sleep. After a little preliminary flyting, the three resolve to sing a catch together, when a voice is heard approaching: the first words uttered, indicate, I think, the sympathies of the author—" Now would God I were in Heaven, for there weep no bairns, so still ! "

The Shepherds ask who goes:

> A man that walks on the moor,
> And has not all his will.

Is it Mak the cattle-lifter? Then let each take heed to his own ! With his quick instinct for a pose, Mak strikes an attitude : I am a King's yeoman, and sent by a great lord, out of my presence, or do me reverence, lest I shall report you.

Now, take out that Southern tooth, say they, it is late, and your name is an ill one. . . . For that, says he, I am true as steel, only my belly fares ill ; an idle, drinking wife, and a house full of bairns, a fresh baby every year !

At last, made free of their fellowship, he lies down to sleep with the rest, only a Shepherd lies on either side to watch his movements. Soon all

H

save Mak are snoring, but to cast them in deeper
slumber, he rises warily and puts a night-spell on
them :

> About you a circle as round as the moon,
> To have done that I will, until it be noon,
> That ye lig there stone-still till that I have doon !
> Over your heads my hand I lift,
> Out go your een and foredo your sicht,
> But yet must I make some better shift,
> And it be right.

Here is a good fat sheep !
This, says he, will I borrow !

Before his own cottage door the thief stands with
his booty :

> How Jill, art thou in ?   Get us some light !
>   JILL.   Who makes such a din this time of the
>   night ?
> I am sat down to spin !

Ah ! is it you my sweeting ?
Come you in ! Now what do I see ! A sheep?
You'll be hanged by the naked neck for this one
day.   Full often you have escaped :

> But so long goes the pot to the water, men says,
> At last
> Comes it home broken !
>   MAK.   Well know I the token,
> But be it ne'er spoken,
> But come and help fast.

They lay their heads together. There is no time
to kill the sheep before the Shepherds are stirring.
Jill will put it in the cradle and say it is a new-
born child, while Mak must hurry back and lie
down in his old place.

Back he goes, and as the others wake, uneasily
asking if anything is wrong, they see the object of
their startled dreams lying sleeping fast between
them. To a shaking he rises, groaning. He has
caught a stiff neck and had a dreadful dream, no
less than that in his absence another child has been
added to his family:—Woe is him has many
bairns, and thereto little bread! I must be going
home. Look up my sleeve and see I've pilfered
nothing.

At home Jill is waiting with a lecture on her
tongue. It is the man, she says, who wanders and
wakes and goes, the woman who brews, and bakes,
and makes new hose; woeful is the household
wanting a woman!

> But what end hast thou made with the herdsmen,
> Mak?

> The last word that they said as I turned my back,
> They would look that they had all the sheep of their
> pack.

Then they will be here anon! Jill will lie in
bed and have the cradle near her. Woman's wit
helps at a pinch, and Mak also knows how to play

his part. Soon they are at the door. Gently he opens it, finger laid on lip :

As far as ye may, good friends, speak softly over a sick woman's head ! Every footstep goes through her ! How wet you all are ! Come in and sit by the fire. Well, my dream was a true one, though there were bairns enough already and to spare. But we must een drink as we brew, and that is reason. You'll dine before you go ?

They decline and hint their suspicions and Mak is outraged :

I stolen your sheep ? You are welcome to search the house ! Shame on you, cries the woman from her bed. Don't you dare come near my bairn. . . . . If you knew, says Mak reproachfully, how it has gone with her, your hearts would ache ! You do ill to come in this fashion— but I say no more ! Peace, poor lass, it fair turns my brain to hear ye !

The search resulting in nothing, the Shepherds a little ashamed, try to make friends. Mak refuses. Only to questions about the new-born babe does he reply that it is fit to be the son of a lord. This histrionic touch is his undoing. At the door, the Shepherds, anxious to make amends, are hunting for a sixpence, and with this humble offering in their hand they ask leave—to kiss the child :

Give me leave but to kiss, and lift up the clout!
What the devil is this? He hath a long snout!
Ay so!
He is like to our sheep,
I trow kind will creep
Where it cannot go!

Jill persists in her story:

A pretty child is he
As sits on woman's knee,
A dilly-down, perdé!

But I was sure that as the
clock struck twelve there was a change! Yes! that
you see is a changeling, and not my child.

Only on a threat of hanging does Mak confess
the truth, and is let off with a tossing in a blanket.*

* The idea of this episode is probably not original to
the playwright.

Then, as all wearily lie down to rest, the Christmas Angel sings of the birth of Christ, and wet with
searching the lost sheep through fen and bog, all
tired and torn as they are, they follow to Bethlehem
and greet the Child:

Lo, but he is merry,
Lo, he laughs, my sweeting!
Ah, the happy meeting—
I have held my promise,
Take this bob of cherries!

Hail! I kneel and I cower, a bird have I brought
To my barne!
Hail, little tiny mop (*bundle*)!
Of our creed thou art crop,
I would drink of thy cup,
Little day-starne!

Hail, darling dear, full of Godhead,
I pray thee be near, when I have need!
Hail, sweet is thy cheer! My heart would bleed
To see thee sit here, in so poor weed,
With no pennies.
Hail! put forth thy dall (*hand*),
I bring thee but a ball,
Have, and play thee withal,
And go to the tennis.

*

*   *

The character of Herod was one of the most important in the cycle. He stood always for the braggart, often over-exaggerated into almost a comedy part. It is Herod who ordains the *Slaughter of the Innocents*, upon which, in the Chester version, dramatic vengeance follows. Among women whose own children have been slain, comes one to whom the child of Herod has been given out to nurse, struck down by his own soldiers:

He was right sicker in silk array,
In gold and pearl that was so gay,
They might have known by his array,
He was a king's own son.

Bootless it is to make moan, to curse and rave at the woman. Gold and gay garb did not save the child, and Herod too must die, and afterward be judged.

Still more impressive, though lacking this episode of the child, is the account of the death of Herod in the Coventry version. Collier has suggested that this is the work of a later hand than the bulk of the plays, but in feeling at anyrate it represents fully the mediæval attitude of mind towards the Intruder.

As Herod's Knights return from slaying the children, their master, to do them honour, commands that a table be spread:

> Covered with a curious cloth, and with rich worthy fare,
> Service for the loveliest lord that living is on ground,
> Best meats and worthiest wines, and look that ye not spare,
> Tho' a little pint should cost a thousand pounds.
>
> My lord, the table is ready dight,
> Here is water, now wash forth right,
> Now blow up minstrels, with all your might,
> The service cometh in soon.

Herod begins to say:

> I was never merrier here before
> Since that I was first born,
> Than I am now, right in this morn,
> In joy I gin to glide.

Mors. Ow! I heard a page make praising of
pride,
All princes he passeth, he weens, in degree,
He weens to be worthiest of all this world wide,
King over all kings that page weeneth to be.
I am Death, God's messenger ;
Almighty God hath sent me here,
Yond' lord to slay withouten fear,
For his wicked working.

Herod is saying to his Knights : Now am I King
alone, my foe is dead, be merry my good Knights.
Yea, they answer, by Satan our sire, it was a
goodly sight when the boys sprawled at the spear's
end; we had been unworthy of your knighting had
we shown them friendship then. . . . He is dead,
says Herod, I doubt not! Minstrels round about,
blow up a merry ditty !
Even as he speaks Death takes him and his
feasters, and the Devil receives their souls :

All ours, all ours! This cattle is mine !
I shall them bring into my cell,
And I shall teach them plays so fine,
And show such mirth as is in Hell.
For in our lodge is so great pine
That none earthly tongue may tell.

Death speaks the epiloogue, a note of grim warning to the audience.

*

*   *

It may be said frankly that the subject of the
Death of Christ is one quite beyond the art of any
of our playwrights in these cycles. All attempts,
and there are many, at realistic representation of
the Agony and the Betrayal, the Trial and the
Crucifixion, are to a modern reader hopelessly
crude and often objectionable. There are passages,
especially those dealing with Mary at the foot of
the Cross, of pathos and some beauty, but on the
whole this series is not very fortunate.

The character of Pilate is generally pourtrayed
with justice and even generosity, as compelled to
yield, protesting to the last, to the High Priest of
the Jews. Especially is this the case in the York
Cycle, in which the incident of the dream of
Pilate's wife is treated very fully and dramatically.

Pilate stands in his chamber listening to the
angry crowd without.

Ye curséd creatures, cruelly crying,

he apostrophises them, as his wife, Dame Percula,
enters to visit him. With her are her damsel and
her little son, and so glad is Pilate of this interruption to painful duties that he has to be re-
minded by his beadle of the hour: Let your wife
go home, says he, the ways are rough, and you have
to sit in judgment on life and limb:

My senior, you see now the sun in your sight,
For his stately strength he stems in his streams,

Behold over your head now he holds from the height
And glides to the ground with his glittering gleams.
To the ground he goes with his beams,
And the night is nighing anon!
Ye may doom after man's dreams,
And my lady here, bright as she seems,
Wightly now let her begone!

The fellow is right, says Pilate, go home, and I
will to sleep. I feel I am tired, lift me on to my
couch, man, and touch me tenderly. . . . Aye, Sir,
says the beadle, you certainly weigh well. . . .
Keep all quiet! Let no one chatter, churl or
child, or to-morrow morn he shall pay for it! . . .
So Sir! Sleep and say no more!

At home Dame Percula is talking with her
maid : Ye are weary, Madam; ye have been a long
way to-day. Get ye to bed. . . . Aye, hap me,
and hence. The little lad shall sleep with me to-
night.

Now the Devil has heard that Christ upon the
Cross shall expiate the sin of Adam and bring
mankind to bliss, and seeks to frustrate the divine
purpose. Stealing to the sleeping woman, he
breathes into her ear : Oh woman, beware and be
wise! The gentleman Jesus unjustly is judged,
and Pilate shall grieve therefor. For his death
shall your strength be destroyed and your riches
reft! Hie to your husband in haste!

She wakes in terror and sends the boy to his
father with the message, but Caiaphas and Annas

are already come there first, and dismiss the story as witchcraft. Beadle, bring him, says Pilate, for I have pity on him. The beadle obeys, bowing himself before Christ:

Wiser wits than mine sang thee Hosannah!

What is this story of Hosannah? queries Pilate, but the priests contradict the beadle till Pilate gives up in despair. Be welcome, he says to Christ, who stands silent before him; and he refuses to observe that the prisoner will do him no reverence: Few are his friends, many his foes; no, cause can I kindly construe why he should lose his life. Lo bishops, why blame ye this boy? Meseems all is sooth that he saith, but ye move all the malice ye may. . . .

As the play proceeds, the supernatural element gains the ascendancy. The lances held by Roman soldiers bow of their own accord as in a salute to the Christ; Pilate, too, is constrained to leave his seat and bend before him. More and more unwilling to doom what seems a demi-god to death, he hesitates and vacillates and compromises. . . . Some lines are lacking from the piece and the reason for his final decision is not obvious.

It would be possible to multiply illustrations of the realism, poetry and legend of these early dramas, but we have yet to consider such isolated

pieces as are not included in the four great cycles,
and space is limited.* Two final examples may perhaps be given : the first, an old lullaby forming
part of the *Slaughter of the Innocents* in the
Coventry Shearmen and Taylor's Pageant; the
second, a lament of Mary the Mother of Christ at
the foot of the Cross, taken from the *Ludus
Coventriæ :*

(1)

Lulla, lulla, thou little tiny child,
By, by, lully, lullay, thou little tiny child,
　　By, by, lully, lullay.

O sisters two, how may we do
For to preserve this day,
This poor youngling for whom we sing,
　　By, by, lully, lullay.

Herod the King, in his raging,
Chargéd he hath this day
His men of might, in his own sight,
All children young to slay.

What woe is me, poor child, for thee
And still I'll mourn and say,
For thy parting, I may not sing
　　By, by, lully, lullay.

* The present volume does not profess to consider
all such pieces but only certain typical examples. To
treat of all the plays, many still in MS, which have
come down to us would be impossible in a work of the
scope and intention undertaken here.

(2)

Oh Son, my Son, my darling dear,
What have I offended thee?
Thou hast spoken to all here,
And not one word thou speak'st to me.

To the Jews thou art full kind
And hast forgiven their misdeed,
And the thief thou hast in mind,
Granting mercy more than meed.

Ah my sovereign Lord, why wilt thou not speak
To me that am thy mother, and painéd for thy
    wrong?
Ah my heart, my heart, why wilt thou not break?
Would that I were hence, from this sorrow is so
    strong!

VII.

THE CORNISH MYSTERIES.

Long after the Mystery Play had lost its vogue in the rest of England, in one forgotten corner of the land it still survived. Even in the days of railroads, Cornwall is hardly part and parcel of England save upon the map. Arched by bluer skies, beaten by wider and more rainbow-tinted seas, the land is set apart, an Avalon of recollections, upon whose sea-front Tintagel yet crumbles. Still more were the Cornish that which the second syllable of Cornwall's name implies—foreigners, like the Welsh—in the days when they yet had a language of their own. Forgotten now, and unspoken, the best specimen of this tongue remains to us in the Guary Miracle Plays of which we are to speak. Quite unlike the English plays are these grave dramatic poems, rich in legend and fantasy, and written for declamation under the open sky. The Theatre, " Round," or *Plaen an guare* in which the performance of the *Guare-mir* took place, was shaped like an amphitheatre, and the actors, in declaiming their long parts were followed by a prompter, book in hand.

The principal Cornish Plays are those translated
by Mr. Edwin Norris for the Clarendon Press.*
They are contained in a fifteenth century MS. in
the Bodleian, and are three in number—*Origo
Mundi, Passio Domini Nostri, Resurrexio Domini
Nostri.* A later play of the *Creation and
Deluge,* written by one William Jordan, in 1611,
is obviously based on parts of the *Origo Mundi,*
and of no particular interest or merit.

In these three plays are contained the principal
episodes of the Old and New Testaments following
closely one upon the other in a series of scenes
without interval. Each play occupied one day,
and the *Origo* and *Passio* end with announcements
of the next day's performance and admonitions to
meditate devoutly the matter of that just ended.

Of the three, perhaps the *Origo Mundi* is the
most interesting and novel, not only in the episodes
introduced, but in the general treatment. The
Creation and Fall of Man, the death of Abel, the
stories of Seth, Noah, Abraham, Moses, David, the
Temple, and Maximilla, treading as the centuries
tread, so fast on one another's heels, with no
interval or blare of trumpeters, are brought into
unity with one another and with the preconceived
plan of the poet, by the adoption of a simple device,
full of imagination. The whole play is, in short,
not so much the story of these men who cross the

* The translation here quoted.

stage from birth to death, as it is the story of that which was before and should be after all of them, the mystical story of the Holy Rood, which is the Tree of Life, which is in certain aspects the Ash-tree Igdrasil.

Not without much persuasion runs the story, did Eve yield to the tempting Serpent, fair-faced as an Angel, and with a voice like a bird in the tree. Not without foreboding did Adam take from her hand the fatal gift, which only threatened forfeit of her love could force him, still reluctant, to accept. Expelled from Eden and driven to toil for bread, his spade, striking the earth, meets but a cry, a cry reiterate with every blow on the un-yielding surface. The earth will not nourish her accursed child, and unless God help him, speedy death is certain. To his prayer God answers:

> Adam, permission shall be forthwith
> To cut the full length of thy spade.
> I command thee, O Earth,
> Allow Adam to open thee!

ADAM.
> O Sire, perfect Lord,
> Little is this for us,
> All that comes, in one day,
> I and my wife shall eat.

GOD.
> Then take two lengths of it
> For thee and thy wife to have.

I

> ADAM.
>
> Lord, this is too little
> If we any children produce.

> GOD.
>
> As need is unto thee,
> Take three lengths of thy spade,
> Athwart measure three breadths,
> And take care not to do falsely.

Ultimately the permission is given, "Go, take all that thou wilt," and the earth becomes obedient to her tiller.

Years pass over, and the two sons of Adam and Eve are growing up to manhood. Cain is not the rough churl of other plays, rather a smooth-spoken hypocrite. He it is who calls on Abel to come and tithe with him. He has no objection to fulfilling the holy rite, only secretly he tries to deceive God, who rebukes him. When his condemnation has been spoken, and Abel praised—Sweet Abel, says he, do not mind all this—all will be well by God's help, the best God of Heaven! Go before me as thou lovest me and—take this, and lie still!

Satan, Lucifer and Beelzebub, beholding this first death, rush to claim for their own the child of fallen Adam and bear his soul to torment, there to remain until the Harrowing of Hell. For his consolation another son is born to Adam, namely Seth. To him he speaks as he feels his life grow a burden more than he can bear. He remembers God's pro-

mise at the time of his expulsion, that in the hour
of his death Oil of Mercy should be given him
from the Tree of Life :

> O dear God I am weary !
> Gladly would I see once more
>   The time to depart.
> Strong are the roots of the briers,
> That mine arms are broken
>   Tearing up many of them.
>
> Seth, my son will I send
> To the Gate of Paradise forthwith,
>   To the Cherub, the guardian,
> Ask of him if there be
> Oil of Mercy at the last,
>   From the Father, the God of Grace.
>
> How shall I find the way to Paradise ?
>
> Follow the prints of my feet burnt ;
> No grass nor flower in the world grows
> In that same road where I went,
>   And we coming from that place.

Guided by such tokens and by the intolerable
flaming of the cherubic sword, Seth comes at last
to the Gate.

What wilt thou here ?   O Angel I will tell thee !
My father Adam is grown old and weary, and
would not wish to live longer—grant me now Oil
of Mercy in his need !

The Angel says, look well within the Gate, say

what thou seest! A fair field I see, woe is him who hath lost it! But the Tree of Life in the midst is dry and dead, parched like those herbs on which my mother and my father set their exiled feet!

O Seth, says the Cherub again, tell me what thou hast seen in Paradise!

Seth answers him:

> All the beauty that I saw
> The tongue of no man in the world can tell it ever:
> Of good fruit and fair flowers,
> Minstrels and sweet song,
>   A fountain, bright as silver,
> And four springs, large indeed,
> Flowing from it,
>   That there is a desire to look at them.

> In it there is a tree,
> High, with many boughs,
>   But they are all bare without leaves,
> And around it bark
> There was none from the stem to the head:
>   All its boughs are bare.

> And at the bottom, when I looked,
>   I saw its roots
> Even into Hell descending,
>   In midst of great darkness.
> And its branches growing up
>   Even to Heaven, high in light.
> And it was without bark altogether,
>   Both the head and the boughs.

CHERUB.

Look yet again within,
And all else shalt thou see,
  Before that thou come from it.

SETH.

There is a serpent in the Tree,
An ugly beast without fail!

CHERUB.

Go yet the third time to it,
And look better at the Tree,
Look what you can see in it,
Besides roots and branches.

SETH.

Cherub, Angel of the God of Grace,
In the Tree I saw,
  High up on the branches,
A little Child, newly born,
And he was swathed in cloths,
  And bound fast with napkins.

CHERUB.

The Son of God was that whom thou sawest,
Like a little child swathed.
  He will redeem Adam, thy father,
With his flesh and blood too,
When the time is come;
  And thy mother, and all good people.
He is the Oil of Mercy
Which was promised to thy father;
Through his death clearly.
Will all the world be saved.

Instructed by the Cherub, Seth returns to his father, and on his death he lays upon his tongue three seeds from the Apple, taken by Eve from the Tree. Adam's soul is also seized by Lucifer and borne to Hell, but from the three pips there spring up three fair saplings. These survive the flood and are found by Moses. Struck with their beauty and fragrance, he cuts them down, and carries them to the house of God where Aaron blesses them. Great is the virtue of the three fair rods. By them the sick are healed and water is smitten out of the barren rock. Before his death Moses plants them again in Mount Tabor, where they take root and flourish, and once more years pass over. The times depart till the throne of David is established in Jerusalem, the King of whose lineage the Messiah must be born. To him appears a vision, bidding him go to the mountain and seek out three fair rods, which he must cut down and bring to Jerusalem, where they will once be needed for a cross. With minstrels and psaltery, viols and lutes, the King rides forth to Tabor on his errand. Once again the rods are cut, once again their fragrance fills the air, once again the sick are healed, the blind, the deaf, and the halt. Of their own accord they root in a green plot and unite into a single comely tree, about whose girth David sets a garland of silver, to count the circles of its growth from year to year. The Tree grows, but the King falls. Bathsheba, washing her robe in

the stream meets his hot love halfway.   At her
instigation he causes the death of Uriah, to spare
her his reproach.   For this Gabriel descends, and
standing before David tells the parable of the one
ewe-lamb, and David, to reconcile God, seeks to
erect a temple to his honour.   The work, left un-
finished by David, is continued by his son, and by
his permission the silver-girdled Tree under whose
boughs David repented his evil, is cut down for the
work.   The sacred nature of the wood reveals itself
in its refusal to fit any part for which the builders
would use it, and it left lying in the Temple as a
relic and curiosity.   Sitting on it, Maximilla finds
herself surrounded with sudden fire, and as her
garments flame from the contact, her heart becomes
inspired, and she prophecies the Christ.   Done to
death for proclaiming new gods, Maximilla becomes the first martyr, while the Tree, now counted
for a piece of wizardry, is taken out of the Temple.
First it is flung into the pool at Bethsaida, which,
ever afterwards, is for the healing of the sick;
secondly, it is laid over Kedron as a bridge; lastly,
it is sought out by the executioners of Christ, and
consents at length to be fashioned into a cross
which had hitherto refused to be fitted to any
service.

In the *Passion* and *Resurrection* are also to be
found features absent from other plays : such are
the refusal of the guilty soul of Judas, after death,
to pass out through the lips which had kissed

Christ; and the suggestion of the Jewish Doctor that Christ can be half God, half man, even as the mermaid is half fish, half woman. Here, too, we learn how, when Christ was to be nailed upon the Cross, the executioner went to the smith in Market Row to buy him nails:

I have none at all, says the smith, and my hands are too sore to make them. . . . They were well enough this morning, says his wife, show them from under your cloak! . . . I will show them willingly — see how the skin is peeled off them! . . . God give thee woe! thou hast worshipped this false knave, and his witchcraft hath done this. Come, I will make the nails! . . . Oh Jesus, says he, be worshipped for thy help! Blessed is he who sets his trust upon thee!

When Christ goes into Hell to fetch away the spirits in prison, his colloquy with Lucifer is adapted from the psalm : *Lift up your heads.* The writing is simple and dignified and not without impressiveness. When the souls are redeemed, straightway they come to Paradise, and enter, and find there Dysmas the thief, to whom Jesus had said thou shalt be with me *this day* in Paradise, and Enoch whom God took, and Elijah the Prophet who was caught up in a chariot of fire.

How came you here, says Adam, and were never in pain with us? Then Enoch and Elijah answer that till this they have not seen death, but that once they must die before Doomsday, and first must they again inhabit the earth.

Alas, says Adam, what will you do there in grief and sorrow? . . . We must needs go in the days of Anti-Christ, to bear witness for the truth. . . . Ah, woe is me! You will come to great disquiet! Do not seek to return to the earth, says poor old Adam, I lived there long in labour and much sorrow. The world is a hard lodging, as I know.

Perhaps the most curious incident in these later plays, is the death of Pilate in the *Resurrection*. Tiberias Cæsar, in his sickness, learns of the prophet Jesus of Nazareth, and sends his messenger to Pilate to make inquiries from him. Now Pilate has newly heard of the disappearance of the body from the tomb, and of the escape of Joseph of Arimathea and Nicodemus, whom he had shut in prison, and being much perplexed and troubled, he merely answers the messenger that he will make diligent search if the man be yet in the land. As he steals away, in comes Veronica, and tells all the truth of the story, and take me, says she, to your Emperor, and my kerchief here shall heal him, for it bears the very image of our Lord. And when she has healed him, she asks no other reward but vengeance upon Pilate. But Pilate bears about him, next his body, one of the garments of Jesus as a charm, and until it be taken from him, none can lay hands on him or do him other than reverence and honour. Pilate, says Cæsar then, I pray you give me that cloth. . . . Now, do not ask me for it! It is not fit for such a lord as you are, and to tell the truth, it has not been washed this long while. . . . Now, give the cloth to me, Pilate! . . . How! to stand naked before so mighty a prince were to do you great dishonour.

Once stripped of the charm he is flung into a dungeon, and overhears how Cæsar and Veronica plot his death together. To all that he can suggest she urges that it is not cruel enough for such a villain as Pilate. So he, to cheat them, stabs himself, and is dead in prison when the tormentors come. Then, earth rejecting his accurséd corpse, it is cast into Tiber, which, because of it, becomes a river of death. Dragged thence with grappling hooks, it must be set forth in an open boat on the high seas, where Lucifer, rising from a rocky island, claims his own.

Needless to say, many of these details were supplied by tradition and by apocryphal Scripture, but their adoption, and the service made of them, are peculiar to the author of these plays. That the plays are by a single author there would seem to be little doubt. They are written in regular stanzas of eight lines with alternate rhymes, occasionally varied with six-line stanzas rhyming, *aab–ccb*, scansion depending on feet and syllables, and not, like the older English verse, on alliterative beats.

The language is throughout dignified and fitting,

and often beautiful. Wherever possible, the words of Scripture have been employed. Thus the later passages of the life of Christ, owe much to the fourth Gospel, while the antiphonal query and response between the angelic hosts and the ascended Christ are based on the prophetic poem : *Who is this that cometh from Edom?* So deeply imbued with the lofty spirit of his subject is the writer of these plays, that these adapted passages are by no means incongruous with such as are original to himself. The whole work is of remarkably uniform merit. From lack of relief supplied by realism and humour, the plays may be regarded as much less dramatic than those of other cycles; but in that atmosphere of pure imagination in which the fountains play and minstrels sing about the Tree of Life, burlesque is impossible, and monotone an artistic necessity; and, on the other hand, the whole work is agreeably free from any enforced moral or conscious didacticism such as too frequently mars the *Ludus Coventriæ*.

VIII.

LATER DEVELOPMENT.

From this brief excursion into the Keltic we return to the study of certain English plays later in date than those of the four great cycles and differing in treatment. Those cycles, it must be repeated, were but examples—probably the best examples—of similar productions popular throughout the country. The primitive simplicity which had demanded them, passed away, the enthusiasm which had inspired them was diverted into new channels, and though new Bible Plays were produced, they were not as the old. So striking, indeed, are the divergences from the earlier type, so new and conflicting the influences exhibited in those plays which date from the end of the fifteenth, and beginning of the sixteenth centuries, that it may be helpful to notice them under their various heads :

1. The older plays are MS. plays intended for acting by various Craft Guilds, and of anonymous authorship. The later plays are printed books published for the reading of the general public,

as well as for acting.   The Digby Plays, which have come down to us in MS. are the only exception to this rule among the examples we are now to consider.

2. The older plays are combined into cycle form, while these treat isolated episodes, no longer as scenes or pageants in an ever moving panorama, but as distinct dramatic themes, considerably detailed and amplified.

3. The older plays sprang directly out of the services of the Catholic Church, were protected and fostered by the clergy and attacked by Lollard reformers.   The later plays are imbued with later doctrine, hint Election and Grace and Down-with-Popery, are indeed, in certain instances, directly propagandist.

4. We find in these later Mysteries the evolution proceeding of that *allegorical* aspect of dramatic action which resulted in the curious short-lived type known as the Morality Play: that tendency to replace the man by the man's most salient characteristic, the human being by the abstract quality, which in the form of prose or poetic allegory has influenced all our literature, and in the legitimate drama has given us Jonson's Humours.

Some, or all of these characteristics we shall find in the plays before us.

*

*   *

The Digby Plays, the earliest of those at present under our consideration, date from the later years of Henry VII. or thereabouts, and exhibit no Protestant influence. There is no suggestion of the old Mystery in their construction, each play treating of a single episode, chosen with regard rather to its dramatic possibilities than to its edifying tendency. At the same time the careful attention to staging and producing, the directions as to costume and effects, prove a development of far greater resources than those at the command of the actor of the cyclical Mystery.

In the *Play of St. Paul,* for instance, we find marginal instructions for storm, thunder, and dances at various moments of the action, nor is the appearance of the actor overlooked : " Here entereth Saul, goodly beseen in the best wise like an adventurous knight." References to " three stations " in this play, coinciding with what we should now regard as the rise and fall of the curtain on three separate acts, might suggest that we have here an early attempt to divide the action of the drama, either by performing its three different parts on three separate platforms, or by the mere announcement at the end of each scene, that the first " station," pageant, or act, was now concluded. This play, like the *Play of Mary Magdalene,* in the same collection, is ascribed, by a handwriting later than the rest of the MS., to Myles Blomefylde, while the play of *Candlemas Day* is similarly

attributed to one John Parfre.　These are the
earliest claimants for dramatic authorship of
Miracles or Mysteries.

The *Play of Mary Magdalene*, written, like that
of *St. Paul* in the East Midland dialect, is a most
unusual combination of Mystery, Allegory and
Romance.　Perhaps it might be reckoned as a
lineal descendant of the old Miracle or Saint's
Play, as differentiated from the Mystery or Bible
Play.　It sums up within itself most mediæval
tendencies, not excluding a little piece of alchemy,
set in the mouth of Mundus, King of the World,
in which is stated the correspondence of the seven
metals to the seven planets.

The story is as follows : Mary of Magdala lives
with her sister Martha and her brother Lazarus,
under the roof of their father, good King Cyrus,
who, feeling death draw near, makes his last will
and testament, and bequeaths his property to his
three children.　After his death, the powers of
evil, seeing his daughter deprived of his good influence, meet in dark conclave, to overthrow her
soul.　To this meeting come the Kings of the
World and the Flesh, the Devil and the Seven
Deadly Sins, a Bad Angel, and a Good Angel, the
latter of whom appears to be present merely as a
listener.　Their plots being laid, the Seven Deadly
Sins besiege the Castle of Magdala, till they make
an entrance for dame Luxuria, "flower fairest of
feminitie."

And how comes it, asks this lady of beautiful Mary of Magdala, that you sit here all alone and see no visitors? . . . My father is just dead, and my heart is heavy for it. . . . You may go too far with that, and fall ill yourself fair maiden. You were better to come with me and see the world! . . . Good-bye, brother Lazarus and sister Martha! Keep my goods till I come home.

In Jerusalem sits a Taverner in his inn and sells white wine and red, both malt and malmsey, claret and many more. Come lady, says Luxuria, here is wine, restorative from care—it won't be a waste of money if we drink some. As they sit at table, there enters a young gallant, Curiosity by name. Is there never a pretty tapstress here to talk to? cries this ancient-modern type; I am the man who likes a girl's hair brushing mine! I've a silk lace for my darling! A sovereign's nothing to me and silk I scorn; nothing shabby about my clothes! My doublet and hose never need to part company! I keep my face clean-shaven and seem for ever young.

This is the man to cheer you! says Luxuria. Come, Taverner, bring him to us.

Ladies, cries the youth, in his affected terms:

> Dear Duchesses and daisies ye,
> Splendid of colour, most womanly,
> Your sovereignity set with sincerity,
> Pray, take my heart your slave to be,
> Or ye pain me with sad perplexity!

J

Do you take me for a street wench? asks Mary
of Magdala.—No, pardieu, my princess! Could
you but know my love!—Your love is very sudden!

> O needs I must, mine own ladye!
> Your person is so womanly,
> I can't refrain, my sweet lily!

Now, says he, will you dance, and then take
sops-in-wine? That I will, sir! I am glad we
met, for I begin to love you. And now, my darling
dear, we have eaten and drunk together, will you
come with me? Yes, to the end of the world, and
be ready to die for you! . . .

The Bad Angel hurries to Hell: Ah, lords, my
lords, hear all at once! She is fallen into sin!
She takes young Curiosity for a king and has done
all his asking! . . .

Mary sits in her arbour, thinking of her lovers
whose number seems to have grown:

> God be with my valentines,
> My sweet birds, my loves so dear!
> My heal they be, and blossom of bliss,
> I marvel none are here.
> But among these balms of price that be
> I will in my arbour bide,
> Till one of them shall come to me,
> To kiss me and sit at my side.

Waiting, she falls asleep, and her Good Angel
steals to her side and exhorts her. She wakes to

repent, to follow Christ to the house of Simon the Leper, and bathe his feet with her tears. Her tender reception by Martha and Lazarus, the death of her brother and his rising from the tomb, confirm her in her piety and her resolve to serve the Christ. Here the first part of the drama closes.

The second part, while following the gospel narrative of the death of Christ and his appearance to the Magdalene in the garden, introduces the story of the King and Queen of Marcylle. The King and Queen are idolators, and their mass is said to Mahound. There are suggestions here that the writer was not unaware of the lax lives of some of the clergy and the abuses of reliquaries. Meantime, Mary, inspired with missionary zeal, has set sail for Marcylle. From the stage directions it would appear that an actual movable ship was to be introduced upon the stage. At the prayer of Mary, the idol and its temple fall to earth, flames break out, and the Presbyter of Mahound descends to Hell. Almost converted, the King promises to become a Christian if Mary can promise to him and his Queen the long, but vainly hoped for child, to inherit his crown. With a saintly smile at the trifling nature of the difficulty, Mary grants his request, and the King and Queen set off together to receive Christian baptism at the hand of St. Peter. In a terrible storm at sea, the child is born, the mother dies, and the shipmen declare that unless the dead body and the hapless child

are cast overboard, all will founder.   The dis-
tracted King lays his loved ones on a ledge of rock,
out of reach of the waves, and kissing them with
tears, continues his pilgrimage. On his return,
behold, wife and child are recovered! More, his
Queen, in spirit, has never left his side, has felt
the hand of Peter on her head, and knelt at Calvary
and the open tomb.   Rejoicing, they return to
offer thanks to Mary Magdalene, and to pray her
ever to abide with them.   But the Saint takes
leave of them here, and obeying a spiritual call,
goes alone into the desert, where she abides in
prayer, fed by angels, until the time of her death.

*

*   *

John Bale, Doctor of Divinity, and sometime
Parish Priest of Thorndon, of Suffolk, wrote four
Mystery Plays, which were printed abroad in 1538.
Bale was the first to apply to such writings the
titles Tragedy or Comedy, and the titles are complete misfits.   He was also the first to divide his
plays into acts, and he wrote rabidly in denuncia-
tion of Catholicism.

Bale's *Tragedy of God's Promises* has been
printed frequently during the last half-century,
his three other Mystery Plays, the *Comedy of
Christ's Temptation*, the *Three Laws of Nature,
Moses and Christ*, and the *John Baptist preaching
in the Wilderness*, are less well known and acces-

sible. Of his historic Morality, *King John*, mention will be made later.

Little can be said as to the intrinsic merit of these works, which are not dramatic and are undoubtedly tedious.

It is rather curious to find in *God's Promises*, a piece dealing with God's compacts for mercy towards mankind as revealed to Adam, Noah, Abraham, Moses and others, a reversion towards the old liturgical type of drama. Each act—and there is an act for every patriarch and prophet to whom the promise is revealed—concluded with directions for a liturgical chant.

For example the scene of Abraham :

Merciful Maker, my crabbed voice direct
That it break out in some sweet praise of thee,
And suffer me not thy due lauds to neglect,
But let me show forth thy commendations free.
Stop not my wind-pipes, but give them liberty
To sound thy name, which is most gracious,
And in it rejoice with heart melodious.

Tune alta voce canit Antiphonam, O rex gentium, choro eandem prosequente cum organis . . . vel Anglice hoc modo.

O most mighty Governor of thy people and in heart most desired, the hard rock and true corner-stone, that of two maketh one, uniting the Jews with the Gentiles in one Church, come now and relieve mankind whom thou hast formed of the hard earth.

It is hardly necessary to contrast this kind of doggerel with the style of the earlier plays. Perhaps the reader will tolerate one brief illustration, after which no more, of Bale's somewhat trenchant method of enforcing his doctrines, illustrated by a passage from the *Temptation*, referring to the Roman clergy :

> What enemies are they that from the people will have
> The Scriptures of God . . .
> And throw them headlong into the devil's dominion?
> If they be no devils, I say there are devils none!
> They bring in fasting, but leave out *Scriptum est*,
> Chalk they give for gold, such friends are they to the beast.

*
* *

Two other plays, the *Interlude of Godly Queen Hester* (published in 1561) and that of *King Darius* (1565)—"a pretty new interlude both pithy and pleasant, imprinted at London in the Fleet Street, beneath the Conduit at the sign of St. John the Evangelist, by Thomas Colwell"—belong to this new school. In the latter, anti-popish doctrines and a prayer for Queen Elizabeth, proclaim those happier times in which freedom of opinion was gradually becoming an integral part of the national heritage.

It is difficult to know how to place these Interludes. They are anomalous developments, halfway between Mysteries and Moralities. They may be considered as Mysteries into which a number of allegorical characters have been introduced, or as Moralities in which a few real men and women are allowed to figure as historical personages. In King Darius the action—if action it may be called when there is none—alternates between scenes of pure allegory conducted by Iniquity, Importunity, Partiality, Charity, Equity, etc., and the story, not a dramatic one, of King Darius and the three men who spoke of the power of the King, the power of wine, the power of women and the power of truth. There is not the slightest connection between the two sets of personages, no attempt made, even to shadow forth, by means of the allegoric figures, the significance of the action of the human characters. Of no value dramatically, this piece cannot be further discussed at present, its abstract personifications, especially its Iniquity, must be considered later in connection with the Moralities.

The *Interlude of Godly Queen Hester* is a stronger and better constructed piece of a similar character. Here, Adulation, Ambition, and Pride, are introduced with the definite purpose of foreshadowing the character of Haman, the theme is in itself strongly dramatic, and the invention of Hardy-dardy is distinctly original. Hardy-dardy, at first the comrade of Ambition and his fellows, next the servant of Haman, and lastly of King Ahasuerus, may be reckoned the first of the famous family of Fools. One thing he lacks, the Fool's

fidelity. Hs is the elvish commentator, whose
folly is better than the wisdom of the wise : One
fool doth well among wise men, he says to Haman;
Ye must needs laugh, and some wise man must
sometimes take the trouble to do on a fool's coat.
His master's fate leaves him merry and moralising :
Now I see that other things need hanging besides
bells and bacon !

> God send all these
> That will steal men's clothes,
> That once they go naked !

With the story of the Bull of Phalaris he wins
Ahasuerus as his patron.

*

*   *

In 1568 there was printed, at London, by Henry
Bynneman, dwelling in Knightsbridge Street, at
the Sign of the Mermaid, a new, merry and witty
Comedy or Interlude, treating upon the *History of
Jacob and Esau*.   The parts and names of the
Players, who "are to be considered Hebrews, and so
should be apparelled with attire," are :

THE PROLOGUE, a poet.
ISAAC, an old man, father of Jacob and Esau.
REBECCA, an old woman, wife to Isaac.
ESAU, a young man and a hunter.
JACOB, a young man of Godly conversation.

JETHAR, a neighbour.
HAMAN, a neighbour to Isaac also.
RAGAN, servant unto Esau.
MIDO, a little boy leading Isaac.
DEBORAH, the nurse of Isaac's tent.
ABRA, a little wench, servant to Rebecca.

The *History of Jacob and Esau* is of its kind
unique. Not since the Towneley Shepherds' Play
of Mak, had there been such an honest attempt to
treat religious drama frankly and humanly. But
this play goes further than the Towneley play,
in so far as its *dramatis personæ* are, for the most
part those of the Bible narrative, its episodes
entirely based upon Scripture. To-day such a
play would probably be prohibited by the censor,
so far have we advanced towards liberty. The
very table of *dramatis personæ* indicates the spirit
of the writer, and the actual characterisation is
far in advance of any previous attempt. Here we
have a real play adapting Hebrew legend much as
Shakespeare adapted Greek and Roman history,
treating Esau, frankly, as " a young man and a
hunter " : inconsiderate, a bit of a bully, loud
voiced, waking up the neighbours with that detest-
able hunter's horn when honest folk are abed,
lovable withal, though too much at the mercy of
his moods—more lovable than the timid sneak his
brother, who prates of being " God's vessel," while
doing what he feels to be a mean and unbrotherly
act. There is something fresh and breezy in the

piece, something of the dewy morning in the wood-
lands, where Esau hunts all day till he is faint,
that intangible effect of sun and sweetness, so hard
to capture in words, so distinctly and supremely
characteristic of the earlier literature of the reign
of the great Queen.   There is humour, too, in this
piece, not the humour of gross contrast, not humour
which to a later age could seem irreverence—for
here the whole action is secular—or sacred—as we
view every-day life, sacred *and* secular as are all
episodes of human existence.   The humour is that
of witty badinage or of situation, and an inherent
quality of the piece.   No divine personage and no
allegorical is introduced, and the didacticism
uttered, sincerely by Isaac, half cantingly by
Jacob, and with unconscious prejudice by the
motherly Rebecca, doting on her younger boy, is
also part and parcel of the characterisation.   The
quality of the piece can be displayed but by illustrations, of which two are appended.   The first is
sufficiently obvious to dispense with explanation;
the second shows the preparation of the broth, in
which is to be seethed, for the misguidance of
blind Isaac, Jacob's kid, instead of Esau's venison.
Both exemplify the method by which the writer
eked out of a scanty theme substance for a five-act
drama, in which, if there be a few long speeches,
there is never any lack of variety of incident.

And with these examples we bid farewell to
English Mysteries and Miracles, and turn for a

little to consider those other didactic dramas called Moralities. Strange and shadowy as dreams the forms that people them! Distorted images of human life, they played brief rôles upon a dusky stage. Vague, mediæval figures, wan as ghosts, survivors of the dim past, startled by cock crow, they made their noiseless exit with the coming of the dawn star of our drama. For it ushered in the day of living things, of quick humanity, and loud-voiced life. And the dawn star and the sun of that bright day was William Shakespeare, with a whole planetary system of clear lights revolving round him in a broader, bluer heaven than night-ghosts wander under.

Actus Secundi, Scæna Tertia.

Mido, *the boy.* Ragan.

[Mido *cometh in clapping his hands and laughing*]
Ha, ha, ha, ha, ha, ha,
Now who saw e'er such another as Esau?
By my troth, I will not lie to thee, Ragan—
Since I was born, I never see any man
So greedily eat rice out of a pot or pan.
He would not have a dish, but take the pot and sup.
Ye never saw hungry dog so stab pottage up.
    Ragan. Why, how did he sup it? I pray thee, tell me, how?
    Mido. Marry, even thus, as thou shalt see me do now.   [*Here he counterfeiteth supping out of the pot*].

O I thank you, Jacob: with all my heart, Jacob.
Gently done, Jacob: a friendly part, Jacob!
I can sup so, Jacob!
Yea, then will I sup too, Jacob!
Here is good meat, Jacob!

RAGAN.　As ere was eat, Jacob!

MIDO.　As e'er I saw, Jacob!

RAGAN.　Esau a daw, Jacob!

MIDO.　Sweet rice pottage, Jacob!

RAGAN.　By Esau's dotage, Jacob!

MIDO.　Jolly good cheer, Jacob!

RAGAN.　But bought full dear, Jacob!

MIDO.　I was hungry, Jacob!

RAGAN.　I was an unthrift, Jacob!

MIDO.　Ye will none now, Jacob.

RAGAN.　I cannot for you, Jacob.

MIDO.　I will eat all Jacob.

RAGAN.　The devil go with all, Jacob.

MIDO.　Thou art a good son, Jacob.

RAGAN.　And would he never have done, Jacob?

MIDO.　No, but still coggl'd in like jackdaw that
　　　　cries *Ka Kob!*

That to be killed I could not laughing forbear;
And therefore I came out, I durst not abide there.

RAGAN.　Is there any pottage left for me that
　　　　thou wot?

MIDO.　No, I left Esau about to lick the pot.

RAGAN.　Lick, quod thou? Now a shame take
　　　　him that can all lick.

MIDO.　The pot shall need no washing, he will it
　　　　so lick;

And by this he is sitting down to bread and drink.

RAGAN.　And shall I have no part with him dost
　　　　thou think?

MIDO.   No, for he pray'd Jacob, ere he did begin,
To shut the tent fast, that no mo' guests came in.

RAGAN.   And made he no mention of me his
servant?

MIDO.   He said thou wert a knave and bade thee
hence avaunt:
Go, shift where thou couldest, thou gottest nothing
there.

RAGAN.   God yield thee Esau, with all my stomach
cheer!

MIDO.   I must in again, lest perhaps I be shent,
For I asked nobody licence, when I went.

Actus Quarti, Scæna Quarta.

ABRA, *the Maid.*   DEBORAH, *the Nurse.*

ABRA.   He, that were now within, should find all
thing, I ween,
As trim as a trencher, as trick, as sweet, as clean;
And seeing that my dame prepareth such a feast,
I will not, I trow, be found such a sluttish beast,
That there shall any filth about our tent be kept,
But that both within and without it shall be swept.

> [*Then let her sweep with a broom, and
> while she doth it, sing this song, and
> when she hath sung, let her say thus:*

The Song.

*It hath been a proverb, before I was born,
Young doth it prick, that will be a thorn.*

Who will be evil, or who will be good;
Who given to truth, or who to falsehood,
Each body's youth showeth a great likelihood,
For young doth it prick that will be a thorn.

[Three more verses follow.

ABRA.   Now have I done, and as it should be for
the nonce,
My sweeping and my song are ended both at once.
Now but for fetting my herbs, I might go play.
Deborah, nurse Deborah, a word I you pray.

DEBORAH *(entering).*   What is the matter?   Who
calleth me, Deborah?

ABRA.   Forsooth, gentle nurse, even I, little Abra.
I pray you, sweet Deborah, take in this same broom,
And look well to all thing, till I return home:
I must to the garden, as fast as I can trot,
As I was commanded to fet herbs for the pot.
But in the meantime I pray you, nurse, look about,
And see well to the fire, that it go not out:
I will amble so fast that I will soon be there,
And here again I trow ere an horse can lick his ear.
[Exit.

DEBORAH.   There is not a prettier girl within this
mile,
Than this Abra will be within this little while.
As true as any steel, ye may trust her with gold,
Though it were a bushel, and not a penny told.
As quick about her work, that must be quickly sped,
As any wench in twenty mile; about her head
As fine a piece it is as I know but a few,
Yet perchance her husband may have of her a shrew.

Cat after kind (saith the proverb) sweet milk will
           lap ;
If the mother be a shrew, the daughter cannot 'scape.
Once our mark she hath, I marvel if she slip—
For her nose is growing above her over lip.
But it is time that I into the tent be gone,
Lest she come and chide me ; she will come now anon.
                               [*Enter* ABRA.

    ABRA. How say ye? Have I not despatched me
      quickly?
A straw for that wench that doth not somewhat
           likely !
I have brought here good herbs and of them plenty
To make both broth and farcing and that full dainty.
I trust to make such broth that, when all things are
           in,
God Almighty self may wet His finger therein.
Here is thyme and parsley, spinach and rosemary,
Endive, succory, lacture, violet, clary,
Liverwort, marigold, sorrel, harts-tongue and sage,
Pennyroyal, purslane, bugloss and borage,
With many very good herbs, mo' than I do name.
But to tarry here thus long, I am much to blame,
For if Jacob should come, I not in readiness,
I must of covenant be shent of our mistress.
And I would not for twenty pound, I tell ye,
That any point of default should be found in me.
                               [*Exit.*

IX.

THE EARLY MORALITY.

The Morality or Moral Play was perhaps the most notable outcome of the mediæval love of allegory. The tendency to express in concrete forms, purely abstract ideas, early influenced poetry and painting, especially in France. *The Romaunt of the Rose* and *The Vision of Piers Plowman,* poems of two worlds, widely sundered, the dream of the lofty-minded courtier and the aspiration of the struggling, submerged peasant, remain to show us how certain ideals leavened all society. Poems both of Life, we may contrast them with that other, sinister allegory, in which all ranks are confounded, the mediæval paintings of the Dance of Death. In reading the one, in regarding the other, we are convinced of the immense influence exerted on the mediæval mind by abstract ideas. Co-existent with this dominance of the Idea, and in no wise conflicting with it, was an insistent realism, an absolute refusal to rest content with vagueness. The age of the Impressionist was not yet. The childlike spirit

K

which asked for pictures of the truths of its religion, applied the same test to ethics, and to all the abstract truths within its grasp.

Man's life is a constant warfare. Standing from birth between his Angels, good and evil, he makes the eternal choice, while hierarchies, celestial and infernal, contend for his allegiance. His youth concedes to follies, which his age, too late, deplores. Last of all Death waits with his sickle in the doorway, the inevitable shadow deepens, and within the shadow is the fire of Judgment. These things are vital, they are of enduring interest. Of them the mind of the Middle Ages said, Let us behold that which we so profoundly believe! Play out before us the battle of these powers, let us see that immanent, abiding Self which is each one of us, and we shall not forget!

An instinct, not wholly morbid, set the skeleton at the old Egyptian feast, the skull and hourglass in the monastic cell, and carved for prelates, yet clothed in carnal pride, those mediæval tombs on which the dead body lies extended, already in its last dissolution, prey of the obscene creatures of the dust. The same instinct set the Dance of Death upon the stage.

This form of drama has been but little studied, and few examples have survived. Creizenach, quoting Seelman, mentions two plays on the subject, one of Lübeck, the other Spanish, and both dating from the fifteenth century. Two French plays are also known to have been performed, one at Bruges in 1449, the other at Besançon in 1453. The Lübeck piece is perhaps typical of a class of representation simple as the old liturgical drama. Pope, king and peasant, each in turn, is beckoned by the bony-handed Death, and while the victim laments his unpreparedness, he is led with dancing steps to the unescapable tomb, and already another follows.

Such pieces seem to have been rare, and we have no trace of their introduction into England in this form. Death is, however, by no means absent from our early drama : he triumphs over Herod and his knights, he summons Everyman when he had him least in mind, he surprises Humanum Genus in the hold of Covetise, but in only one play shall we find his coming the matter of the piece. In England, as elsewhere, the subject was probably too grim for popularity, and the majority of the Moralities, especially the earlier ones, deal with the story of Mansoul, the old strife between Good and Evil.

To consider, or even to enumerate, all the dramatic renderings of this theme which belong to the years between the accession of Henry VI. and the death of Elizabeth, would be here impossible. In its later developments it underwent many modifications, and we need not be surprised to find allegorical drama a weapon in the hands of sectarians, and even politicians; while the undeniable fact that even wickedness has its humour, led to a class of plays, bordering closely on Comedy. The earliest examples are, however, faithful to the original ideal, and present in dignified and not undramatic form the life of man, the pigmy immortal, whose soul is coveted of the great conflicting powers. Dealing strictly with this subject, and never deviating into humour or topical allusion, are three great Moralities, *The Castle of Perseverance*, *Everyman*, and *The World and the Child*.

The Castle of Perseverance is the finest, and most ancient, of three Moralities contained in what is known as the Macro MS., and is generally considered our earliest extant Morality. It is written in the East Midland dialect, which has given us so many of our early literary specimens, and may date from the reign of Henry VI. In the same MS. as the play is a rough sketch of the scene—a Castle in the centre of two circles, one enclosing the other. Over the Castle is written: "This is the Castle of Perseverance, that standeth in the midst of the place, but let no man sit there, for letting of sight, for there shall be best of all." Underneath the Castle is a bed, with the direction: "Mankind his bed shall be under the Castle, and there shall the Soul lie under the bed till he shall rise and play." As the cue for *Anima* to appear, occurs only towards the end of this long drama, we can imagine that the part was no light penance.

We read also that "Covetise' cupboard by the
bed's feet, shall be at the end of the castle."
Within the double circle we are to understand a
moat, and without it are five scaffolds for God,
Covetise, the World, the Flesh and the Devil.
Against the scaffold of Belial, in the north, we
have the odd directions as to his appearance,
quoted earlier; and, in addition, the injunction
that Mercy shall wear white, Righteousness, red,
Truth, sad green, and Peace, black.   The play
seems to have been cried a week beforehand by two
Vexillators, or Flag-bearers, setting forth its contents in alternate stanzas, and exhorting attend-
ance "this day sevennight at —— on the green,
at underne of the day."

The piece opens by the World, the Flesh, and
the Devil, proclaiming from their various scaffolds
their rule and potency, and their intention to des-
troy Mankind.   Immediately afterwards, Mankind
(*Humanum Genus*) appears as a little new-born
child between his good and evil Angels.   Beguiled
by the latter, he stands before the World, and in
the presence of Lust-and-liking, and Folly, swears
to him allegiance.   Here he is richly clad, and
sent with Backbiter to Covetise, the treasurer of
the World.   Covetise hails him, and instructs him
how he shall live:

> Thou must give thee to Simony,
> Extortion and false assize;

> Help no man but thou have why,
> Pay not thy servants their service;
> Thy neighbours look that thou destroy,
> Tithe not, on no wise;
> Hear no beggar tho' he cry,
> And thou full soon shalt rise.
> And when thou usest merchandise,
> Look that thou be subtle of sleight,
> And also swear by all deceits,
> Buy and sell by falséd weights,
> For that is kind covetise.

Avarice calls in the rest of the Deadly Sins, and the Good Angel of Mankind weeps in despair. To his aid comes Shrift, who, as usual in these pieces, has no difficulty in convincing Mankind, now a man of forty, of his folly, and leads him from his ill companions into the Castle of Perseverance and the society of the Virtues. But the Bad Angel is also watchful. He betakes him to Flibbertigibbet Backbiter, and bids him warn his masters:

I go, I go, says he——

> I go, I go, on ground glad,
> Swifter than ship with rudder;
> I make all men mazed and mad
> And every man kill other.

This is the messenger of evil who goes unsaid saws to say, and makes a third to every two. He does his errand well, crying in the ears of the three potentates, that their children, the Deadly Sins, have played them false, and Mankind has escaped.

At once the great battle is set against the Castle.
The Devil and the Flesh with their grosser allied
Sins are defeated, but the World remains, and in
his ranks, foremost is Covetise. Generosity, seeing
him approach, strives to repel him—"Damsel digne
on dais," answers he, " I speak not right to thee."
With him alone Mankind descends to parley, and
having parleyed, yields. He leaves the Castle, not
without regrets, and follows Covetise, who promises
riches untold and teaches him to adopt henceforth
as motto, " More and more." He grows old in
hoarding and hugging ill-gained wealth, and
Covetise remains faithful to his pact. But now
Death enters and deals a bitter blow, and when the
old man cries upon the World, for old acquaintance sake to help his need——What, says the
World, has Death been speaking with thee? I
cannot help thee then! Time thou wert in thy
grave and another had that was thine! Our bond
of love is broken, and thou, like the rest, shalt yet
be caged in cold clay. . . . Go, boy, he cries to one
who stands for the rising generation, take yon'
man's goods for thy inheritance!——And who are
you? says the old man to the young intruder.
What is your name? You are not of my kith
and kin, have never done me service!——I am the
World's page, and my name is I-wot-never-who!
——Then for I-wot-never-whom have I laid up
rents and lands, and purchased parks and goods,
with care and strife, this many and many a day!

The poor Soul rises now, and reproaches the wastrel body on the bed—for whose brief pleasure, she must suffer endless pains. She appeals to God, but the Devil mocks her prayer, describes her coming torment, and bids her follow him.   In Heaven, meantime, is enacted the old scene, Justice and Truth, disputing with Peace and Mercy. God awards His judgment with the latter, Mankind is rescued from doom, and sits in Heaven at the right hand of God, in bliss.

This play, type of so many that were to follow it, is a sufficiently coherent and dramatic composition.   The construction is good, and the brief dialogues between the good and evil Angels, recurring at certain crises with the regularity of the Greek Chorus, serve to mark the acts or stages of the piece.

The idea of representing the hero, Mankind, at various ages, was a favourite device, and we find it again employed with great effect in the play of the *World and the Child.*

This piece, printed by Wynken de Worde in 1522, belongs by tone and construction to the earlier and more dignified period of the Morality. Its date may be earlier than that of the published edition, probably about 1500.   In this play, Mankind, represented first as an infant, stands before Mundus, the great King, begging for food and clothing in exchange for which he swears his fealty.   Mundus grants his request, gives him gay garments, names him Wanton, and bids him, when fourteen years of age, return to him. The child goes away, whips his top, fights brother and sister, and plays truant from school, and when seven years have gone returns again to Mundus. Mundus gives him new garments and a new name, Lust-and-liking, and tells him he shall follow

> All game and glee and gladness,
> All love-longing in lewdness;
> This seven year forsake all sadness,
> And then come again to me.

Lust-and-liking goes away again, "fresh as flowers in May, and seemly shapen as the same," clad in royal attire, and dazzling the eyes of ladies. At twenty-one he goes again to Mundus, who expresses his approval. Like God, Mundus will make man in his own image:

> I increase thee in all thing,
> And mightily I make thee a man:
> Manhood-mighty shall be thy name.
> Bear thee prest in every game,
> And wait well thou suffer no shame,
> Neither for land nor for rent.

Seven Kings there are who do Mundus service, they are the Seven Deadly Sins, of whom Gluttony is to be chiefly avoided as bringing to poverty and Lechery to be followed, while Pride, Envy and

Wrath are not to be disdained. After this valuable counsel, dubbing him a knight, and arraying him fittingly, Mundus exhorts Manhood-mighty to be constant in his allegiance:

> And here I dub thee a knight,
> And haunt alway to chivalry:
> I give thee grace and also beauty,
> Gold and silver great plenty,
> Of the wrong to make thee right.

Manhood goes about, bragging his power and his fame. He almost fancies that he is greater than Mundus. While his boasts are at their prime, Conscience enters and accosts him. . . . And what will you of me? says Manhood. Anything consistent with Pride? . . . Nay, sir, beware of Pride, by whom Lucifer fell, remember also Robert of Sicily, that proud king! . . . . What say you then to Lechery, with whom I love to linger? . . . . Nay, flee from Lechery ere you be brought to misery! . . . . And what of the rest, then? What of Covetise?

> Sir, Covetise in good doing
> Is good in all wise!

Yea, Covetise is a king to be obeyed, so thou covet to keep God's law, covet to slay no man, to steal nothing, to honour father and mother . . . . And leave all game and glee? . . . Nay, mirth in measure is good for thee. . . . . Measure, what is measure? . . . To live in charity and eschew all folly. . . . And what is folly? . . . To obey the Seven Deadly Sins I tell you of. . . . Nay, thou liest! Mundus told me these were kings!

Left alone to meditate, Manhood resolves to combine the service of Conscience, whom he respects, with that of Mundus, who is very useful to him. His resolution is tested by the sudden entrance of Folly, who, not without difficulty, obtains his hearing: Come with me to the taverns, and then for other adventures, for you know such things are but manhood. . . . Yes, but I would not have Conscience see me! . . . Have no fear: you shall say you are not Manhood, and change your name to Shame. . . .

Old, decrepit, wretched, Manhood returns from following after Folly. He has a new name, Age, and his prayer is for Death to free him. His prayer is heard by the friend of Conscience, Perseverance, who names him anew, Repentance, receives his lamenting confession, and prepares him for the end.

By its simplicity and the symmetry of its construction, the *World and the Child* conveys a more complete and harmonious impression to the reader than does *The Castle of Perseverance* with its many characters and quickly succeeding incidents. But it is probable that for acting purposes the latter, by virtue of its constant movement, would be much more successful. There is little incident in

the *World and the Child*, and until the entrance of
Conscience, such incidents as constitute the play
are of a parallel or recurrent nature, and follow
one another as identically as the following waves
of the tide.

In *Everyman*, probably the greatest, certainly
the most impressive of the Moralities, the author
does not attempt to depict the whole of life, nor
even a lengthy period. An unerring instinct leads
him to select one, great, dramatic moment, in the
realisation of which, all that has been before, all
that may be thereafter, is, inevitably, recollected
and foreshadowed.   For the vision of Death in-
cludes the panorama of Life.

Everyman, though first printed at a later date
(c. 1500—9) may be as old as the reign of Edward
IV., and in its whole atmosphere is distinctly
mediæval.   The Introduction states the matter:

> Here beginneth a treatise how the high Father of
> Heaven sendeth Death to summon every creature to
> come and give account of their lives in this world
> and is in manner of a Moral Play.

God in Heaven looks down upon mankind, and
perceives all living without thought of Him:

> I see the more I them forbear,
> The worse they be from year to year;
> Needs on them must I do justice,
> On Everyman living without fear:
> Where art thou, Death, thou mighty messenger?

DEATH.

Almighty God, I am here at your will,
Your commandment to fulfil.

GOD.

Go thou to Everyman,
And show him in my name
A pilgrimage he must on him take,
Which he in no wise may escape,
And that he bring with him a sure reckoning,
Without delay or any tarrying.

. . . . . .

EVERYMAN.

What desireth God of me?

DEATH.

A reckoning will He needs have:
On thee thou must take a long journey,
Therefore thy book of count thou with thee bring,
For turn again thou cannot, by no way,
Therefore be sure of thy reckoning,
For before God thou shalt answer and show
Thy many bad deeds, and thy good but a few,
How thou hast spent thy life, and in what wise,
Before the chief Lord of Paradise.

EVERYMAN.

Full unready am I such reckoning to give!
I know thee not: What messenger art thou?

DEATH.

I am Death, that no man dreadeth.

EVERYMAN.

O Death, thou comest when I had thee least in mind!
In thy power it lieth me to save,
Yet of my goodwill I give thee, if thou be kind,
Yea, a thousand pounds shalt thou have
And thou defer this matter to another day!

.   .   .   .   .   .

DEATH.

Everyman, it may not be, by no way . . .
For an I would receive gifts great,
All the world might I get;
But my custom is clean contrary.
I give thee no respite: come, hence, and not tarry.

EVERYMAN.

O gracious God in the high seat celestial,
Have mercy on me in this most need!
Shall I have no company in this vale terrestial
Of mine acquaintance that way to lead?

.   .   .   .   .

FELLOWSHIP.

Everyman! good-morrow, by this day!
Sir, why lookest thou so piteously?
If anything be amiss, I pray thee me say,
That I may help to remedy.

.   .   .   .   .   .

For in faith and thou go to Hell,
I will not forsake thee by the way.

EVERYMAN.

Commanded am I to go a journey,
A long way, hard and dangerous,
And give a straight account, without delay,
Before the high judge Adonai.

FELLOWSHIP.

If we took such a journey,
When should we come again?

EVERYMAN.

Nay, never again till the day of doom.

FELLOWSHIP.

For no man that is living to-day,
I will not go that loathsome journey!

EVERYMAN.

Gentle Fellowship, help me in my necessity!
We have loved long and now I need,
And now, gentle Fellowship, remember me!

FELLOWSHIP.

Whether ye have loved me or no,
By St. John, I will not with you go!

    .   .   .   .

EVERYMAN.

Where be ye now my friends and kinsmen? Lo,

    .   .   .   .

My Cousin, will you not with me go?

COUSIN.

No, by our Lady!

    .   .   .   .   .   .

EVERYMAN.

Ah Jesu! is all come here to?
Lo, fair words maketh fools fain!
What friend were best me of to provide?
All my life I have loved Riches,
I will speak to him in my distress.
Where art thou my Goods and my Riches?
I have thee loved, and had great pleasure,
All my life days, on Goods and Treasure.

GOODS.

That is thy damnation without lesing,
For my love is contrary to the love everlasting.
For a little while I was lent to thee,
A season thou hadst me in prosperity:
Weenest thou that I will follow thee?
Nay, not from this world, verily!

Forsaken and refused of all, Everyman remembers his Good Deeds. They lie, " cold in the
ground " and fettered by his sins, but from their
captivity exhort him to seek out Knowledge, by
whom he shall be helped to make his reckoning.
From Knowledge to Confession, from Confession
to Penance, from Penance to the Priest and the
last unction, Everyman goes step by step to the
verge of the grave. Here is the last denial, the
ultimate desertion. Strength, Beauty and Discre-
tion quit him there, and leave him to his fate:

Yet I pray thee, for love of the Trinity,
Look in my grave once, piteously!

Nay so nigh I will not come,
Farewell fellows everyone!

Last an Angel takes the pardoned soul into celestial peace, and the play concludes with a warning
epilogue.

It has seemed best to relate the matter of this
piece as far as possible in the author's words, than
which none could be more simple and impressive.

This play of *Everyman* is the only drama of its
kind which we possess, standing in direct relation
to the Dance of Death.   Its nationality has indeed
been called in question, since it is in many respects
identical with the Dutch play of *Elckerlijk*
(= Everyman) dating from the same period.   A
translation seems beyond question, but hitherto
the question of priority has not been decided, and
it may be that each has derived from some common
original now lost.   These are students' matters.
For the general reader the play's the thing.   It is
indeed unique and arresting as befits its great subject, Death.   The majority of the Moralities deal,
as already indicated, with life and its temptations.
Of such nature are *Lusty Juventus, Youth, Hick-
scorner, Mankind, Wisdom,* and many others.   In
these the interest lies in the strife between good
and evil in the heart of man.   Repeatedly, in varying phrase or form, they challenge Life to bear the
scrutiny of conscience.   Hypocrisy, convention,
hardness-of-heart, stupidity and folly, have known
in all ages how to ignore, mock, or evade the
challenge.   There is another challenge before
which all these are confounded, it is the challenge
of *Everyman,* which is the challenge of Death.

*

*   *

The contemplation of eternal truths is, after
all, no pastime, and the idea of entertainment is
inseparable from the theatre.   With a foregone

L

conclusion, however delayed or disguised, interest is apt to pall. In the end, familiarity with evil breeds contempt or tolerance. It is impossible to deny that virtue may be dull, and vice, not un-amusing. The writer of the very inferior Macro Morality of *Mankind*, though not daring to depart from the conventional position, manages to render Mercy despicable, while the assailing vices are commended to the injudicions of his audience by a species of foul-mouthed humour. The ultimate triumph of virtue hardly conceals the writer's sympathy with the opposers.

The punishment or consequence of crime lies within the domain of Tragedy. In Comedy it is legitimate to depict a laughing virtue or to " sport with human follies." It is a still more necessary relief to the action of Moral Plays, and the dramatic instinct of the early playwrights evolved a character especially to fill this rôle, namely the Vice.

The Vice is almost peculiar to English Morali-ties, and became in time the Fool of Shake-speare's plays. His figure, absent from such early and dignified examples as *Everyman*, and the *Castle of Perseverance*, appears for the first time in such Moralities as border upon Comedy, while in one later instance he enlivens a Miracle Play—*King Darius*, printed in 1565.

The Vice, who frequently appears in company with the Devil, is the jester of the Satanic court,

the impish setter-on to evil, the humorous commentator. It was his part to skip upon the stage,
fantastically clad, whipping out with the dagger
which he bequeathed to Harlequin.

> *I am gone, sir,
> And anon, sir,
> I'll be with you again,
> In a trice,
> Like to the old Vice
> Your need to sustain.
>
> Who with his dagger of lath,
> In his rage and his wrath,
> Cries, ah, ha! to the Devil,
> Like a mad lad,
> Pare thy nails dad;
> Adieu, good man devil.

" It was a pretty part in the old Church plays "—
so runs a passage in *Harsnet's Popish Impostures*
(1603)—"when the nimble Vice would skip up
nimbly like a Jack-an-apes into the Devil's neck,
and ride the Devil a course and so belabour him
with his wooden dagger till he made him roar."

Ben Jonson, who introduced Satan and the
Vice, Iniquity into the first scene of *The Devil is
an Ass*, makes the former complain that the old-
fashioned Vice is out of favour now: it might

---

* *Twelfth Night.*

make a Lady Mayoress laugh if old Iniquity were
to skip upon the table and leap into a custard, but
would scarce catch souls for Hell. The modern
vices are "most like to virtues," and subtler wiles
must be employed "to keep us in credit."

In the *Staple of News*, he again refers to the
subject:

> My husband, Timothy Tattle, God rest his poor
> soul! was wont to say there was no play without a
> Fool and a Devil in't; he was for the Devil still, God
> bless him! The Devil for his money, would he say,
> I would fain see the Devil. . . .

> But was the Devil a proper man, Gossip?

> As fine a gentleman of his inches as I ever saw
> trussed to the stage or anywhere else; and loved the
> Commonwealth as well as ever a patriot of them all:
> he would carry away the Vice on his back quick to
> Hell, in every play where he came and reform abuses.

*

*   *

King Darius is probably older than the printed
edition, and in that case we may regard it as the
earliest piece in which the Vice is actually referred
to as such. On his first entrance he begins:

> How now my masters, how goeth the world now?
> I came gladly to talk with you,
> But soft, is there nobody here?
> Truly I do not like this gear.

Ah whoreson knaves, have you thus me mockéd?
Surely I will break their head!
Come not near, it were for you best,
If you do, it shall not be for your rest——

With much more such doggerel. When Charity
enters, clad as an ancient father, he threatens him
with his dagger:

Therefore get thee quickly away,
Or with my dagger I will thee slay.

To Equity he says: What! have we more *blesseds*
come to town? Go play with my mother's pussy-
cat or I will lay my dagger about thy pate.

In *Trial of Treasure* (printed 1567) the Vice is
played by Inclination, who incites the hero, Lust,
to set his heart on Treasure and Pleasure, both of
whom, in the day of need, forsake him. None the
less he is a mischievous, rather than a malicious
knave, and his comments are shrewd and true. As
Pleasure and Treasure swear their constancy—You
are both as constant, he mutters, as snow in the
sun.

He enters with a jargon of nonsense:

I can remember since Noah's ship
Was made and builded on Salisbury Plain,
The same year the weather cock of St. Paul's caught
    the pip,
So that Bow-bell was like much woe to sustain.
I can remember, I am so old,
Since Paradise Gates were watched by night:

And when that Vulcan was made a cuckold,
Among the great gods I appeared in sight.
Nay—for all your smiling I tell you true!
No, no! ye will not know me now,
The mighty on earth I do subdue—
Tush!—if you give me leave, I'll tell you how.

The broad comedy effect of this character seems
to have been heightened by investing his clown-
visage with enormous spectacles, and the wooden
dagger was inseparable from the rôle.

Such personifications stand on the border-line of
Comedy, and it is not surprising to find plays of
the period in all but name belonging rather to
Farce than to the Morality proper.

Such pieces are *Tom Tyler and his Wife,* not
printed till 1661, but ascribed by the publisher to
a much earlier date—"a hundred years ago,"—and
that excellent comedy, *Jack Juggler,* printed about
1562.

In *Tom Tyler,* the part of Vice is assigned to one
Desire, by whose inciting he has been led to marry
Strife. Desire has nothing of the buffoon about
him. He argues with Destiny—"a sage person"—
their respective shares of responsibility in Tom's
affairs, and most unhappy marriage. Strife is a
drunken shrew who gossips with Tipple, the ale-
wife, and gets thrashed on her husband's behalf
by Tom Taylor, a working man. If these characters belong to Morality so may Volpone and
Morose, Sir Politick-would-be, Doll Common, and

Ananias Tribulation. Only after study of this earlier dramatic period can we thoroughly appreciate the place of Jonson's plays.

The exact significance of *Jack Juggler* is less easily defined. It appears at first that which the prologue expressly and with curious insistence declares of it—mere comedy, a thing only to make you merry :

> And such a trifling matter, as, when it shall be done,
> You may report and say you have heard nothing
>   at all;
> Therefore, I tell you all, before it be begun
> That no man look to hear of matters substantial,
> Nor matters of any gravity, either great or small,
> For this maker* showed us that such manner things
> Do never well beseem little boys'† handlings.

The play reveals no more, but the epilogue hints at some occult and hidden meaning :

> Somewhat it was, saith the proverb old,
> That the cat winked when her eye was out;
> That is to say, no tale can be told,
> But that some English may be picked thereof out,
> If so to search the Latin and ground of it men will
>   go about;
> As this trifling interlude that before you hath been
>   rehearsed
> May signify some further meaning, if it be well
>   searched.

* The writer of the play.
† Often the actors of these pieces.

Such is the fashion of the world now-a-days,
That the simple innocents are deluded,
And an hundred thousand divers ways
By subtle and crafty means shamefully abused,
And by strength, force and violence oftimes compelled
To believe and say the moon is made of a green
    cheese,
Or else to have great harm and per case their lives
    lese.
And in every faculty this thing is put in ure,
And is so universal that I need no one to name,
And, as I fear, is like evermore to endure,
For it is in all faculties a common sport and game,
The weaker to say as the stronger biddeth or else to
    have blame,
As a cunning sophist will by argument bring to pass
That the rude shall confess and grant himself an ass.

If, as has been suggested, an attack on the
Roman Church be here intended, it is curious that
at this date it should need such careful disguise.
In *King Darius* the Vice claims the Pope as his
father, and with Elizabeth on the throne, such
caution seems unnecessary. The piece may be
older than its published version, or may hide some
purely topical allusion impossible now to trace.

The comedy itself (and, as Hazlitt said, the
allegory won't bite) is a clever one. It is one of
our earliest plays of confused identity. Jack
Juggler, the Vice, having an old grudge against
Jenkin Careaway, Master Bongrace's page-boy,
takes an opportunity to disguise himself in his

likeness, and stand at Bongrace's door like a servant of the house. Now Bongrace is from home, at a feast, and has bidden Careaway go as fast as he can to his wife and bid her join him. Careaway, going at his own pace,* which permits of many adventures, arrives to find his double at the door, who first beats him for his audacity in announcing himself as Careaway, and afterwards proves his case by relating to the bewildered page-boy all that he has been doing through the day. Quite forgetful of his errand, and terribly confused, the latter retreats to think where he can have " lost his self," and when he ventures back, the double has disappeared. In his place, however, Mistress Coy, with her maid, waits him, and from these he receives such handling for his absence and his "lies" about his double, that he is fain to take to flight. Meantime, Master Bongrace returns to inquire after his wife, and, to excuse his negligence, Caraway pours his story of the double into his sceptical ear.

Why, thou naughty villain, says Bongrace, dost affirm me that which is impossible?

That one man may have two bodies and two faces,
And that one man may be in one time in two places?
Tell me, drankest thou anywhere by the way?

That I did not, says the boy, no meat has been

* *"As fast as a bear in a cage."*

mine but blows.   Had I as many meals as beatings
I were well fed.   I know it was I and no other.
He told me all I had done since you sent me on
your errand. . . . And what was that? . . . Why,
says the unwary one, walking into the trap:

How I did at the bucklers play,
And when I scattered a basket of apples from the
    stall,
And gathered them into my sleeve all,
And after that how I played also. . . .

But here Nemesis brings down the curtain, and
the play comes to an inevitable ending.

PROTESTANT MORALITIES.

Plays in favour of the Reformation, even, oddly enough, in strong advocacy of puritanic doctrine, are not lacking among the Moralities, while two early pieces deal respectively with politics and science, unusual themes, in England, for the drama.

The first of these, *Albion, Knight,* may date from the reign of Henry VIII. It is, unfortunately, in the only copy known to be extant, very fragmentary, and it is difficult to learn the trend of the argument. The date of the piece is therefore much less easy to decide. Albion is, of course, England, while such characters as Injury, Justice and Division, indicate the nature of the subject. Injury's enumeration of the difficulties which attend the passing of any measure of reform might apply to later days:

Sir, ye ought to be contented best of all
Where Justice is treated with due equity,
And where no favour nor meed should be,
And when Reason hath tried there every deal
That such an act were good for the Commonweal.

If therein any loss may be
To the disadvantage of Principality,
Such an act loseth all his suit,
With a little inducing of reason astute.
And if it touch the Lords Spiritual,
Or be disadvantage to the Lords Temporal,
Farewell go-bet (*reform*)! This Bill may sleep
As well as through the Parliament creep.
And if that merchants be moved withal,
Or any multitude of the Common Hall,
'Tis not for us, say they then,
This Bill is naught but for to wipe a pen,
And this is all your new equity,
And for all your message, thus will it be.

The *Interlude of the Four Elements*, printed
about 1500, is a remarkable attempt to popularise
the science of the day. It treats of divers matters
relating to natural science : Of the situation of the
four elements; of certain conclusions proving that
the earth must be round; of the cause of the ebb
and the flood of the sea; of the cause of the light-
ning, of blazing stars, and flames flying in the
air, etc.

How dare men presume to be called clerks,
Disputing of high creatures celestial,
As things invisible and God's high works,
And know not these visible things inferial?
So they would know high things, and know nothing
     at all
Of the earth here whereon they daily be,
Neither the nature, form, nor quantity.

In place of God, so often the opener of Mysteries
and Moralities, we have here Nature, the wise
guardian and first instructor of Humanity.
Studious Desire and Experience continue his
education and the conflict between their claims
and the allurements of Sensual Appetite and his
crew of merry-makers, forms the action of the
play. Seduced from his first allegiance, Humanity
runs to a tavern with his new-found boon companions. Here he is promised acquaintance fitting
his mood: Little Nell, a good dancer, Jane with
the black lace, bouncing Bess, and two or three
proper wenches more.

While he is rollicking here, Experience, widely
travelled, relates in a somewhat lengthy colloquy
his tidings and adventures to Studious Desire. A
most interesting reference is made at this point to
the newly-discovered continent across the Western
Sea, a land yet conjectural and unexplored:

> This sea is called the Great Ocean,
> So great it is that never man
> Could tell it since the world began,
> Till now within this twenty years
> Westward be found new lands,
> That we never heard tell of before this
> By writing nor other means;
> Yet many now have been there.
> And that country is so large of room
> Much larger than all Christendom
> Without fable or guile.
> For divers mariners had it tried,

And sailéd straight by the coast side,
About five thousand mile!
But what commodities be within,
No man can tell, nor well imagine;
But yet, not long ago,
Some men of this country went,
By the King's noble consent,
It for to search, to that intent,
And could not be brought thereto.
But they that were th' adventurers
Have cause to curse their mariners,
False of promise, and dissemblers,
That falsely them betrayed.
Which would take no pains to sail further,
Than their own list and pleasure,
Wherefore that voyage and divers other
Such caitiffs have destroyed.
Oh what a thing had be then,
If they that be Englishmen
Might have been the first of all
That there should have take possession,
And made first building and habitation
A memory perpetual!

If the passages between Humanity and his tutors
are apt to fall into a little tediousness, those in
which he follows his less reputable friends are full
of life and vigour.   At one point the "philo-
sophers" are routed by Ignorance, and Humanity
re-claimed by his former boon companions. Come,
says Ignorance, the audience is tired of your prat-
ing with that knave Experience,

For all that they be now in this hall,
They be for the most part my servants all.

At this point it would seem that a ballet takes place. The dancers enter, and while they dance they sing. This would go better to music, says Sensual Appetite, and humming a stave of the song, hurries away to fetch minstrels. . . . Let us sing a ballad till he comes again, says Humanity. . . . Nay, sir, answers Ignorance, none of your prick-card song for me, for God's sake!

> HUMANITY. Peace man! prick-song may not be despised,
> For therewith God is well pleased,
> Honoured, praised and served
> In the Church oftimes among.
> IGNORANCE. *Is* God well pleased trowest thou thereby?
> Nay, nay, for there is no reason why!
> For is not as good to say plainly
> *Give me a spade,*
> As *Give me a spa...ve...va...ve...va...ve...vade?*
> But if thou wilt have a song that is good,
> I have one of Robin Hood,
> The best that ever was made.

Then follows the mock song of Robin Hood, perhaps our earliest example of nonsense rhyme, a jumble of phrases from ballad and romance:

> Robin Hood in Barnsdale stood,
> And leant him till a maple thistle;
> Then came our Lady and sweet St. Andrew—
> Sleep'st thou, wak'st thou, Geoffrey Coke?

A hundred winter the water was deep,
I cannot tell you how broad :
He took a goose neck in his hand,
And over the water he went.
He start up to a thistle top
And cut him down a bollen club,
And struck the wren between the horns,
That fire sprang out of the pig's tail.
Jack boy, is thy bow i-broke?
Or hath any man done the wriguldy wrag?
He plucked *muscles out of a willow
And put them into his satchel!
Wilkin was an archer good,
And well could handle a spade;
He took his bent bow in his hand,
And set him down by the fire.
He took with him sixty bows and ten,
A piece of beef, another of bacon.
Of all the birds in merry England,
So merrily pipes the merry bottle.

Students of early Drama and Poetry would do
well to compare this burlesque with Peele's *Old
Wive's Tale*.

It is to be regretted that the *Interlude of four
Elements* has come down to us imperfect, and that
its conclusion is left doubtful. It would appear,
however, to take the form of a wise compromise
between Studious Desire and Sensual Appetite,
sanctioned and approved by Nature. In such a
conclusion, however, the author of the play stands

* *Mussels?*

almost alone, and the day was coming in which the writers of Moral Plays must have defeated their own purpose by the rigidity of a doctrine to which lenience was perdition and Nature, Antichrist.

*

*   *

The Morality Play proper of the reign of Elizabeth—the Morality Play which disguised neither farce nor topical allusion under allegoric nomenclature, but remained faithfully didactic— was, as a rule, most strongly puritanic.   Such pieces are out of all sympathy with the general trend of early Elizabethan literature.   True, we have *Euphues* and *Arcadia*, high ideals of pure living and noble thought, but these, like most of the literature of the age, are suffused with sunshine.   The puritanic Moralities are a little out of the picture.   Perhaps for this reason the lament of the playwright in Greene's *Groatsworth of Wit* (1592).

> But now my almanac is out of date,
> The people make no estimation
> Of Morals teaching education.

The puritanic tendency made itself evident, indeed, at a much earlier date.   The reign of Edward VI. was a brief summertide beguiling many blossoms that were blighted in the wintry days that followed.

M

The play of *Lusty Juventus*, written about 1550,
by one Richard Wever, of whom nothing else is
known, illustrates the extreme narrowness of the
teaching of the new morality, and calls to mind a
passage, set in the mouth of the adversary, in another puritanical play : *

> Since these Genevan doctors came so fast into this
>   land,
> Since that time it was never merry with England.

The meeting between Lusty Juventus and Good
Counsel opens thus :

LUSTY JUVENTUS.

Well i-met father, well i-met !
Did you hear any minstrels play
As you came hitherward upon your way ?
An' if you did, I pray you wish me thither,
For I am going to seek them, and by my faith I
    know not whither.

GOOD COUNCIL.

Sir, I will ask you a question by your favour:
What would you with the minstrel do ?

LUSTY JUVENTUS.

Nothing but have a dance or two,
To pass the time away in pleasure.

* *New Custom.*

GOOD COUNCIL.

If that be the matter, I promise you sure,
I am the more sorrier that it should so be,
For there is no such passing of the time in Scripture,
Nor yet there unto it doth not agree.

The play of *New Custom*, written early in the
reign of Elizabeth, might be reproduced to-day
and serve as a topical exposition of more recent
disputes among divines, learned and otherwise.

The piece deals with one, nick-named, but
wrongly, says the writer of the play, New Custom,
a preacher in London, young and daring.

In London, not long since, you wot well where,
They rang to a sermon, we chanced to be there:
Upstart the preacher—I think not past twenty year
    old,
With a sounding voice, and audacity bold,
And began to revile at the Holy Sacrament and
    transubstantiation!
    .   .   .   .
What! young men to be meddlers in divinity! It is
    a goodly sight!
Let us alone with divinity which are of riper age,
Youth is rash, they say, but old men hath the
    knowledge.

They have brought in one, a young upstart lad as it
    appears,
I am sure he hath not been in the realm very many
    years,

ı a gathered frock, a polled head, and a broad
hat,
unshaved beard, a pale face: and he teacheth
that
All our doings are naught, and hath been many a
day,
He disalloweth our ceremonies and rites, and teacheth
another way
To serve God than that which we do use.
He goeth about the people to abuse—
'Tis a pestilent knave. . . .
And to term him by his right name, if I should not
lie,
'Tis *New Custom,* for so they do him call,
Both our sister Hypocrisy, Superstition, Idolatry
and all;
And truly methinketh they do justly and wisely
therein,
Since he is so diverse and so lately crept in.

1565—1907—one section of humanity remains
unchanged and unchanging.

*

* *

We come now to a point at which the Morality
touches and merges in the Drama proper.

John Bale, writer of several Mysteries, was
author also of a historical drama, vindicating the
memory of *King John.* Catholic in his youth,
Bale became a Protestant under Edward VI., lived
abroad during the Marian persecution, and re-
turned, Prebend of Canterbury, when Elizabeth

succeeded. Ardently, even bitterly zealous for re-
formed religion, John, who had quarrelled with
the Pope of Rome became to him a hero, and his
play was written to prove that all his actions were
inspired by his chivalry towards the widow, England. Clergy, Civil Order, Sedition (the Vice or
Jester), the Papal Legate, the Pope Innocent III.,
and Stephen Langton, are some of the characters
of this medley piece. It occupies a curious position between Morality and Tragedy, for it ends
with the poisoning of John by the Monk of Swin-
stead Abbey.

Like the rest of Bale's plays, *King John* is very
tedious, and a little unconvincing. A reference to
Henry VIII. as " that Duke Joshua which brought
us into the land of milk and honey," commends the
author's policy rather than his veracity, and even
the play of *King John* leaves the reader unsatisfied
as to the absolute integrity of its hero.

In two other early plays, both ascribed to a date
prior to Mary's accession, Tragedy bears the impress of the Morality. *The Disobedient Child*, and
(possibly) *The Nice Wanton* are the work of one
Thomas Ingeland, one time student at Cambridge,
of whom no more is known.

Properly speaking, these plays belong to the
regular Drama, but since both are purely didactic,
and written to enforce certain moral teachings, we
may consider them briefly in this connection. In
the first the Devil plays a kind of entr'acte, while

in the second, the Vice Iniquity brings the two spoiled children to ruin. The sister dies in shame and poverty, the brother "hangeth in chains and waveth his locks."

Such plays remain to prove that a certain influence for good was, after all, exerted on the national Drama by the Morality. Dryden, in his preface to the *Conquest of Granada*, lays down the rule that in every dramatic piece there must be a *moral*, that is an underlying and unifying thought about which the play is constructed and of which it is an illustration. But the writers of the Moralities did not, in general, anticipate this truth. One moral, that it is better to serve good than to serve evil, was the theme of countless plays, and the species degenerated inevitably into artificiality and dullness. There was hope for a writer like Ingeland in whose two dramas virtue is *not* triumphant, who dares to let the curtain descend on ruin or unavailing repentance. Such a writer touched the confines of the loftiest drama, the drama of which the glorious flower was Faust. But these exceptions were few, and it will be noted that this little group of plays stands midway between the Moralities of Catholic, and those of Protestant conviction. The new enthusiasm for the new religion, set the moralists off on the old road again, but with a difference—the triumph of the Good was still their theme, but the Good became identified with their own private opinions.

How far English dramatic literature has been
influenced by the Morality, is difficult to say, but
one thing is certain—the regular Drama was never
evolved therefrom. Touch as they may here and
there, the two are innately opposed. The Drama
must be, however, imperfectly and dimly, the
mirror of life as it is; the Morality is the mirror of
life as the moralist thinks it should be—and how
small a world, and how cold, is compassed in its
sphere!

An interesting pamphlet, Willis's *Mount Tabor*
(1639) recalls the performance of that popular
Morality, *The Cradle of Security*, of which no
copy is known to be extant. The passage may permit of quotation, and admits of transformation as
we read—for so perhaps to watch the Mysteries at
Kenilworth, William Shakespeare stood, a little,
wondering boy, between his father's knees :

> In the City of Gloucester the manner is (as I
> think it is in other like corporations) that when
> Players of Interludes come to town, they first attend
> the Mayor, to inform him what nobleman's servants
> they are, and so to get licence for their public
> playing ; and if the Mayor like the Actors, or would
> show respect to their Lord and Master, he appoints
> them to play their first play before himself and the
> Aldermen and Common Council of the city ; and that
> is called the Mayor's play, where every one that will
> comes in without money, the Mayor giving the
> Players a reward, as he thinks fit, to show respect
> unto them. At such a play, my father took me with

him, and made me stand between his legs, as he sat upon one of the benches, where we saw and heard very well. The play was called the *Cradle of Security*, wherein was personated a King or some great Prince, with his Courtiers of several kinds, among which three Ladies were in special grace with him, and they, keeping him in delights and pleasures, drew him from his graver Counsellors, hearing of sermons, and listening to good counsel and admonitions, that, in the end they got him to lie down in a cradle upon the stage, where these three Ladies, joining in a sweet song, rocked him asleep, that he snorted again, and, in the meantime, closely conveyed under the clothes wherewithal he was covered, a vizard like a swine's snout upon his face, with three wire chains fastened thereunto, the other end whereof being holden severally by those three Ladies, who fall to singing again, and then discovered his face, that the spectators might see how they had transformed him, going on with their singing. Whilst all this was acting, there came forth of another door at the farthest end of the stage, two Old Men, the one in blue, with a Sergeant-at-arms his mace on his shoulder, the other in red, with a drawn sword in his hand, and leaning with the other hand upon the other's shoulder; and so they two went along in a soft pace, roundabout by the skirt of the stage, till at last they came to the cradle, when all the court was in greatest jollity, and then the foremost Old Man with his mace struck a fearful blow upon the cradle, whereat all the Courtiers, with the three Ladies, and the vizard, all vanished, and the desolate Prince, starting up barefaced, and finding himself thus sent for judgment, made a lamentable complaint of his miserable case, and so was carried

away by wicked spirits. This Prince did personate
in the moral, the Wicked of the world, the three
Ladies, Pride, Covetousness and Luxury, the two
Old Men, the End of the World and the Last Judgment. This sight took such impression on me, that
when I came towards man's estate, it was as fresh
in my memory, as if I had seen it newly acted.

CONCLUSION.

The ethical drama, Mysteries, Miracles and Moralities, passed with the growth of the great secular drama. Mediævalism passed with it, and a certain chapter in stage history, was closed which has not been since re-written. The Theatre was, for good and ill, denationalised, and became henceforth a profession.

Looking back, we pause to ask what was the place and influence of this once potent, but now effete tradition—in literature, in dramatic art, in daily life? What vestiges of its practice yet survived its disappearance?

Influence is a thing so subtle that it is impossible to completely summarise its workings. It is secret, evasive, and, above all, unconscious. It is not enough to tabulate obvious instances, to point to Ben Jonson's *Humours* as survivals of the old Morality, to Milton's *Comus* and *Samson Agonistes*. It does not suffice to say that Biblical drama, imported from France, and allegory, unknown to our earliest national literature, were especially adapted to that deep strain of seriousness and moralising which some consider our peculiar racial endowment, for all over Europe the same forms were popular.

The religious drama doubtless had its influence on art and also on life, but that influence is not to-day very clear and definite.

For the most part the dramatists of the Elizabethan period turned for their inspiration to new sources, especially where Tragedy was concerned. The writers, indeed, of some of our early secular plays, exhibit a crudity of characterisation, a feebleness of construction, which had learned little or nothing from the better examples of the religious theatre. When we turn to consider Comedy, however, we find in the earliest and most truly native examples just the characters, the dialogue, the situations, which had delighted the audiences of the Mystery Plays. The Comedy of Manners is not native to our soil; the wit of Sheridan, like the wit of Shaw, is essentially non-English. The native English notion of Comedy is to be studied in *Gammer Gurton* and *Ralph Roister Doister*, its products are Nick Bottom, Dogberry and Verges, Launce and his dog Crab. And the elements of this kind of humour, of this far from exquisite fooling, this frank taste for a broadly funny situation, are all to be found in the Mysteries as they are in Chaucer's poems.

Perhaps the Mysteries did as much for the audience as for the dramatist. Their enactment through centuries, above all their enactment *by the people*, had made the Theatre a national tradition, and it was inevitable that with the new life of the Renascence, there should be a new Theatre, and a public waiting for it.

That Theatre, as we know, was the outcome of differing, almost conflicting influences, native and classic, popular and literary. We have to thank the native and popular drama for that free development which braved the classic unities and discarded Senecan tradition. These wanderings over sea and land, these lapsing years in which Perdita grows from babyhood to womanhood, and kings establish great conquests before laying down the sceptre—what were they to those who had watched on some rude platform, earth, heaven and hell from the Creation to the Cross?

When we turn to consider the influence of the religious drama on the life and thought of the people, we are in reality considering a wider question, the influence of the Bible on the national character. For the religious theatre was, in its first and most potent period, simply the people's Bible. Its existence and growth were proof, not of its own influence, but of that enthusiasm for the Scriptures, that eager desire for familiarity with their teachings, that, in a later age, regarded these very makeshift representations of the Stage as almost blasphemous, and demanded, no more illustrations, but the text, the book itself. None the less, these illustrations had been well adapted for fulfilling a certain purpose, had stimulated interest and excited desire, had been not without value in instructing the childish mind, scarce able to spell out letters. Having accomplished their unconscious destiny, they passed. The Mystery Play disappeared, the Morality followed soon after, but the Authorised Version of the Scriptures was given to the country to exercise a wider influence and appeal to a larger public than was possible to any earlier translation.

Here and there in country districts, old customs lingered on. But such customs, divorced from the ritual and teachings of the Catholic Church, were no longer powerful as means of instruction and admonition.

One such instance is quoted in Disraeli's *Curiosities of Literature* in the article on the *State of Religion during our Civil Wars*, in which John Shaw, Vicar of Rotherham, relating his ministry among a good and ignorant congregation in Cartmel, Lancashire, is quoted as follows :

I found a very large and spacious church, scarce any seats in it, a people very ignorant and yet willing to learn, so as I frequently had some thousands of hearers. I catechised in season and out of season. The church was so thronged at nine in the morning that I had much ado to get to the pulpit. One day an old man, about sixty, sensible enough in other things, and living in the Parish of Cartmel, coming to me on business . . . I desired to be informed of his knowledge of religion. I asked him how many Gods there were? He said he knew not. I, informing him, asked again, how he thought to be saved? He answered he could not tell, yet thought that was a harder question than the other. I told him that the way to salvation was by Jesus Christ, God-Man, who, as he was man, shed his blood for us on the Cross. Oh, Sir, said he, I think I heard of that man you speak of once in a play at Kendal, called Corpus Christ's Play, where there was a man on a tree, and blood run down, etc. And afterwards he professed he could not remember that he ever heard of salvation by Jesus but by that play.

Such survivals were, however, infrequent; the secular drama was in full blossom of splendid vitality, the Bible Play was out of date and out of fashion; it belonged to an earlier, simpler, and much smaller world, and was moreover regarded as a relic of Popery. Could it have survived the rivalry of the Elizabethan and Jacobean Theatre, that stage of present pulsing, multi-coloured life, whereon the triumph and power of the world, the beauty and might of the flesh, the splendour of strong, swift action, not always in the cause of the right, excluded those pallid, phantom figures which had peopled the old Moralities, and incorporated even Sin, even Repentance, even Death in the scheme of crowded, eager, vivid experience, set gigantic vices and overwhelming destructions as the bitters at a feast of what variety, what wonder, and yet always a feast!—had the

religious drama survived this potent rival with
its intimate appeal to the life that now is in each
and every man, it must have inevitably yielded to
the new religion, the more complex, inquiring,
rationalising thought of the age, the turmoil of
civil war and the strife of the sectaries.   It
could not survive, any more than yesterday can
survive to-day, and for the same reasons.   It did
not attempt to survive, and the deterioration, attendant on a species which has outlived its day,
was, to a great extent, avoided.

In the eighteenth century, however, a curious,
sporadic form without art or dignity flourished for
a while, and obtained popularity both in England
and abroad.   This was the religious Puppet Show,
to which numerous allusions are to be found in the
literature of the period.

Powell, the Puppet Showman, is mentioned frequently in the *Tatler* and *Spectator*.   We have
references to a Puppet Show of the Creation, to
advertise which, " the puppet drummer, Adam and
Eve, and several others that lived before the flood,
passed through the streets on horseback to invite
us all to the pastime."   Later a " new opera,
Susanna, or Innocence betrayed," is promised for
" next week, with a new pair of Elders."

In 1780, Mickle, translator of Camoen's *Lusiad*,
wrote from Lisbon : " Beside the Opera there is
another playhouse, where they act what they call
Precipos or Scripture Histories."   He then pro-

ceeds to describe a play by puppets, " before a crowded and pretty genteel audience," the programme including the War of the Angels, Adam and Eve, Noah, etc., concluding with scenes from the New Testament.

In France, the acting was not confined to puppets. Moore's *Fudge Family in Paris* refers to these very popular dramas which attracted large crowds to see the Passage of the Red Sea, and Daniel among the Lions:

> The next place (which Bobby has near lost his heart in)
> They call it the Playhouse—I think—of St. Martin ;
> Quite charming—and *very* religious—what folly
> To say that the French are not pious, dear Dolly,
> When here one beholds, so correctly and rightly,
> The Testament turned into melodrames nightly.
> And doubtless, so fond they're of Scriptural facts,
> They will soon get the Pentateuch up in five acts.
> Here Daniel, in pantomime, bids bold defiance
> To Nebuchadnezzar and all his stuffed lions,
> While pretty young Israelites dance round the Prophet,
> In very thin clothing, and but little of it.
> Here Bégrand, who shines in this Scriptural path,
> As the lovely Susanna, without even a relic
> Of drapery round her, comes out of the bath,
> In a manner that, Bob says, is quite *Eve-angelic!*

The Puppet Show remained popular till a late date. In 1822 Michelet, editor of the *Mirroir* was prosecuted for having outraged the religion of the

N

state by publishing a letter from Dieppe entitled
Travelling Shows.

*You remember, says the writer of this letter, to
have seen at St. Cloud certain tents in which
monkeys, learned dogs, and other phenomena are
shown to persons who feel interested in these matters.
Walking on the port the other day with friends I
proposed that we should enter a tent of this kind to
see what animals it contained. . . . Approaching,
we heard the crier, a trumpet in his hand, calling
to the people, and with the voice of a Stentor,
announcing that the show would commence immediately, and that it would be still more wonderful
than any that had before been exhibited. Walk in,
said he, ladies and gentlemen ! You will see the
Birth of our Saviour, the Doubts of Joseph about
the Virgin Mary his wife, the Passion, the
Resurrection, etc. We rushed in and obtained the
front seat without caring for the price, which,
however, was full sixpence. The curtain was soon
drawn up, and I saw all the family of Punch,
transformed to Jews, Pharisees and Magicians . . .
Joseph . . . called his spouse some hard names that
mightily pleased the audience . . . You see, said a
married woman who sat behind me, that the injustice
of husbands preceded the birth of the Saviour.
    The Passion followed . . . and the show . . .
finished with the Resurrection. The spectators
retired, cracking a thousand jokes upon the puppets
transformed to Jews and Romans, and I for a
moment imagined myself carried back to the remote

* Quoted by Hone.

period of which Boileau speaks, when an ignorant troupe of strollers represented Mysteries on temporary scaffoldings.

In Germany, Tableaux were also presented, accompanied by fitting music, and it may be, as Hone suggests, that the ancient Mystery gave rise to the Oratorio.

From Puppet Shows and melodramatic spectacles, it is pleasant to turn to those few genuine survivals of the religious drama, which yet remain to-day.

The Passion Play of Oberammergau is still a sacred mystery, a true act of worship. Whatever it may be to a large portion of its motley audience, to its actors and producers it remains a tremendous symbol. Monopolised by no profession, it yet embodies the devout instinct of a simple peasantry, and all such embodiments, even in their cruder forms, stand high, untouched by that greatest foe of art, vulgarity.

Here and there the old spirit, the old practices survive, and wherever they do so, they bring with them a breath, a whisper of something forgotten, something remembered, as the perfume of byegone springtides greets us from the last unfolded violet.

In southern lands, customs from the Corpus Christi and similar processions yet survive. In Lent and Holy Week every statue is draped in mourning, a dramatic desolation broods over the gloomy church. The shrine of the Madonna is yet garlanded for the Nativity. The Bambino lies smiling in the manger cradle, and from olive grove and hillside, herdsmen and peasants come to make their offering.

As it was in the beginning—the love of the Symbol is deep-rooted in the very essence of our consciousness, and is not to be eradicated. Not while we have in us imagination, curiosity, reverence, or call it what we will, that apprehension gilded by some fugitive gleams of knowledge, of a surrounding mystery to which our own life, above all our moral development, stands in some close, yet undiscerned relation.

STUDENTS' LIST.

EDITIONS.

The *Early English Text Society* publishes:
The Chester Plays.
The Coventry Plays (re-edited from the edition
of Thomas Sharp, 1825).
The Digby Plays.
The Towneley Plays.
The Macro Plays.

The *Shakespeare Society* publishes:
The Ludus Coventriæ,
and has editions of some of the Plays published later
by the E.E.T.S.

The *Clarendon Press* publishes:
The York Plays,
with an excellent introduction to the subject by Lucy
Toulmin Smith.
English Miracle Plays, Moralities and Interludes,
Selected and edited by Alfred W. Pollard. A first
handbook for every student.

The *Early English Drama Society* publishes:
The Dramatic Writings of Richard Wever and
Thomas Ingelend (*i.e.*, Lusty Juventus, The
Disobedient Child and The Nice Wanton).

The Anonymous Plays series (3 vols.), including
Everyman, King Darius, Jacob and Esau,
New Custom, Trial of Treasure, etc., etc.

Hazlitt's Dodsley's Old Plays
Contains the majority of the Moralities referred
to in this book.

The *Plays of Bale* are published as follows:
God's Promises. Dodsley, vol. i.
Also in Selected Miracle Plays published by
Wm. Marriott, Basel and Paris, 1838.
The Temptation of Our Lord, ed. by the Rev.
A. B. Grosart in the Miscellanies of the
Fuller's Worthies Library, vol. i. (1870).
John Baptist Preaching in the Wilderness,
in the Harleian Miscellany, vol. i.
King John, ed. by J. Payne Collier in the Camden
Society's publications.

For the *Cornish Plays, vide,*
The Ancient Cornish Drama,
Translated and edited by Edwin Norris,
Univ. Press, Oxford.
The Creation of the World, a Cornish Mystery,
Translated and edited by Whitley Stokes,
Williams and Norgate, London and Edin-
burgh, 1864.

AUTHORITIES.

Borlase: Natural History of Cornwall.
Carew: Cornwall.
Chambers, E. K.: The Mediæval Stage.

*Le Clerc et Renan : Historie Littéraire de la France au quatorzième Siècle.

Collier, J. Payne: English Dramatic Poetry and Annals of the Stage.

Creizenach: Geschichte des neueren Dramas.

Hone: Ancient Mysteries.

Julleville, Louis Petit de: Littérature Française.

Morley, Henry: Sketch of English Literature.

Morley, Henry: English Writers.

*Paris, Matthew: Vitæ Vigintitrium Sancti Albani Abbatum (vol. 1., p. 56. Edn. folio of 1640).

*Parker: Glossary of Architecture (art. Sepulchre).

Sharp, Thomas: A Dissertation on the Pageants or dramatic Mysteries anciently performed at Coventry by the trading companies of that city (Coventry, 1825).

Symonds, John Addington: Shakespeare's Predecessors in the English Drama.

Ten Brink: English Literature, vol. ii.   Bohn's Edition.

Ward, A. W.: A History of English Dramatic Literature.

* For reference only.